i

EMPOWERING INDUSTRY WITH AI: STRATEGIES FOR SUCCESS

Harnessing Generative AI to Drive Industry Transformation

Rick Abbott

The measure of intelligence is the ability to change.
— Albert Einstein

Ethics is knowing the difference between what you have a right to do and what is right to do.
— Potter Stewart

To the visionaries and change-makers who dare to push the boundaries of technology and redefine what is possible.

PREFACE

In the annals of technological innovation, few advancements have captured the imagination and potential of human ingenuity as profoundly as Generative AI (GenAI). From its nascent beginnings in academic laboratories to its current transformative applications across industries, GenAI has rapidly emerged as a game-changing force—a technology capable of reimagining creativity, amplifying productivity, and addressing challenges once thought insurmountable.

This book, *Empowering Industry with Generative AI – Strategies for Success*, is both a guide and a vision. It is designed for business leaders, technologists, policymakers, and innovators seeking to harness the power of GenAI to create value, enhance efficiency, and solve complex problems. The emergence of GenAI, encompassing technologies like large language models, image generators, and advanced predictive systems, marks not just a technical revolution but a paradigm shift in how we think about work, innovation, and human-machine collaboration.

We are at the precipice of a new industrial revolution. Just as steam engines powered the Industrial Age and microprocessors fueled the Digital Era, GenAI is poised to become the transformative engine of our time. Unlike its predecessors, however, GenAI doesn't just execute tasks or process information; it creates, augments, and collaborates. It can design new products, write compelling narratives, forecast market trends, and even generate solutions to problems we have yet to define. It is not merely a tool—it is a collaborator, one that complements human creativity and decision-making.

The journey of integrating GenAI into industries is both exciting and complex. Organizations must navigate a landscape filled with opportunities and challenges. For every breakthrough in efficiency or innovation, there are critical questions to address: How do we ensure ethical AI deployment? How can we mitigate biases embedded in data? What strategies will help businesses maximize value while minimizing disruptions? These are not peripheral concerns; they are central to the responsible and effective adoption of this transformative technology.

This book is structured to guide readers through this journey. It begins by laying a strong foundation, exploring the origins of artificial intelligence, the capabilities and limitations of GenAI, and the ethical considerations that must underpin its deployment. From there, it delves into industry-specific applications, offering practical insights and real-world examples of how GenAI is reshaping sectors such as healthcare, manufacturing, retail, and government. These chapters highlight not only the technology's potential but also the strategies and frameworks needed to implement it effectively.

Central to this book is the belief that the integration of GenAI is not just a technical challenge but a human one. It requires visionary leadership, cross-functional collaboration, and a commitment to upskilling the workforce. The chapters on implementation strategies and organizational readiness are designed to equip leaders with the tools they need to drive transformation while fostering trust and engagement among employees and stakeholders.

As we look to the future, the possibilities of GenAI are boundless. Emerging trends such as multimodal AI, enhanced explainability, and democratized access to advanced models promise to unlock new opportunities for innovation. At the same time, they underscore the need for vigilance, adaptability, and a firm commitment to ethical principles.

The title of this book reflects its dual purpose: to inspire and to instruct. *Empowering Industry with Generative AI – Strategies for Success* is not just about understanding what this technology can do; it is about understanding how to use it effectively, responsibly, and strategically. It is about charting a course for organizations to navigate the complexities of this new frontier, transforming challenges into opportunities and ideas into impact.

I invite you to embark on this journey, to explore the transformative power of GenAI, and to consider how it can shape not only industries but also the very way we think, create, and connect. The future is unwritten, and GenAI is one of the pens with which we will write it. Let's begin.

TABLE OF CONTENTS

INTRODUCTION: GENERATIVE AI IN INDUSTRY

Artificial intelligence has long been a focal point of technological advancement, inspiring both fascination and apprehension. From the early days of symbolic logic and rule-based systems to the rise of machine learning and neural networks, AI has continuously evolved to meet the demands of an ever-changing world. Today, we find ourselves at the cusp of a new era: the era of GenAI. Unlike its predecessors, which excelled at processing and analyzing data, GenAI possesses a remarkable ability to create—whether that means generating text, producing images, composing music, or even designing entire systems. This creative capacity opens a wealth of opportunities for businesses to innovate, differentiate, and thrive.

What Is GenAI?

GenAI refers to artificial intelligence systems that can generate novel content based on patterns and data they have been trained on. Unlike traditional AI, which focuses on classification, prediction, and optimization, generative models specialize in producing new and often surprising outputs. At the heart of this capability are technologies like Generative Adversarial Networks (GANs), Variational Autoencoders (VAEs), and large language models like OpenAI's GPT series.

What makes GenAI so revolutionary is its ability to mimic human creativity. For example, it can write compelling articles, design marketing materials, and even create prototypes for physical products. By automating tasks that were once thought to be uniquely human, GenAI is not only enhancing productivity but also redefining what is possible in the business world.

Why GenAI Matters for Businesses?

In today's hyper-competitive environment, businesses are constantly seeking ways to stand out. GenAI provides a powerful tool to do just that. Its applications span virtually every industry and function:

- **Marketing and Advertising:** Imagine launching personalized campaigns at scale, each tailored to the preferences of individual customers. GenAI can craft engaging content, design visually stunning ads, and even predict customer responses to marketing initiatives.
- **Customer Experience:** AI-powered chatbots and virtual assistants can provide personalized and immediate support, improving customer satisfaction and loyalty.
- **Product Development:** Whether it's designing a new product or optimizing an existing one, GenAI can streamline the creative process by offering innovative ideas and simulations.
- **Operations and Efficiency:** From automating routine tasks to generating optimized workflows, GenAI is transforming how businesses operate, reducing costs while improving outcomes.

Yet, with all this potential comes complexity. Businesses must not only understand the technology but also navigate the ethical, legal, and practical challenges it presents. This book aims to equip you with the knowledge and tools to do just that.

The Paradigm Shift

The advent of GenAI represents more than a technological breakthrough; it signifies a paradigm shift in how we think about creativity, innovation, and problem-solving. For decades, businesses have relied on humans to drive ideation and execution, while machines handled repetitive and analytical tasks. GenAI blurs these boundaries, enabling machines to contribute meaningfully to the creative process.

Consider, for example, how GenAI has transformed industries like entertainment and fashion. In Hollywood, AI tools are being used to generate storyboards and write scripts, offering new possibilities for storytelling. In fashion, AI-generated designs are hitting the runways, showcasing styles that push the boundaries of conventional aesthetics. The same principles apply to more traditional industries like manufacturing, healthcare, and finance, where GenAI is being used to design equipment, develop treatment plans, and even create trading strategies.

The Challenges Ahead

While the opportunities are immense, the path to successfully integrating GenAI is not without obstacles. Organizations face several key challenges:

- **Data Dependency:** GenAI models require vast amounts of high-quality data to perform effectively. Securing and managing this data can be a significant hurdle.
- **Ethical Concerns:** GenAI can inadvertently produce biased, misleading, or harmful outputs. Ensuring fairness and accountability is critical.
- **Regulatory Landscape:** Governments and regulatory bodies are only beginning to grapple with the implications of AI-generated content. Businesses must stay ahead of evolving compliance requirements.
- **Integration Complexity:** Implementing GenAI is not as simple as flipping a switch. It requires thoughtful integration with existing systems, processes, and culture.

This book addresses these challenges head-on, offering insights into how businesses can navigate them while maximizing the benefits of GenAI.

A Roadmap for Readers

The chapters that follow provide a comprehensive exploration of GenAI and its impact on business. The journey begins with a historical overview of artificial intelligence, setting the stage for a deeper understanding of how we arrived at this pivotal moment. From there, we delve into practical frameworks, ethical considerations, and detailed applications across key business functions such as marketing, finance, operations, and talent management.

This book is organized into 14 chapters that explore the potential opportunities, limitations and drawbacks, and practical guides for implementing GenAI in your organization. Each chapter examines a different industry and demonstrates how GenAI can enhance, complement, or challenge established approaches:

- **Chapter 1: A Brief History of Artificial Intelligence** traces the evolution of AI from ancient myths to modern GenAI, highlighting key milestones, challenges, and lessons that set the stage for its transformative potential.
- **Chapter 2: Introduction to Generative AI in Business** introduces the transformative potential of GenAI in business, highlighting its diverse applications, capabilities, and ethical considerations.
- **Chapter 3: Ethical, Legal, and Regulatory Considerations** examines key considerations of deploying GenAI, emphasizing the importance of addressing bias, ensuring transparency, protecting privacy, complying with regulations, and establishing robust governance frameworks to responsibly integrate this transformative technology into businesses.
- **Chapters 4-12:** explore the potential for leveraging GenAI in key Industries such as Manufacturing, Health Case, and Education.
- **Chapter 13: Implementing GenAI in Your Organization** provides a comprehensive roadmap for organizations to effectively adopt, integrate, and maximize the value of GenAI technologies.

- **Chapter 14: Future Trends** explores future trends in GenAI, highlighting advancements in natural language processing, image and video generation, and context understanding, alongside their transformative impacts on industries and the challenges of ethical, privacy, and regulatory considerations.

Setting the Stage

GenAI is more than a tool; it is a catalyst for transformation. It challenges us to rethink the boundaries of human and machine capabilities and to reimagine the way we work, create, and connect. As you read this book, I encourage you to think broadly about the opportunities and challenges ahead. What role will GenAI play in your industry? How can it enhance your organization's mission? And, most importantly, how will you ensure that its benefits are realized responsibly and equitably?

The journey into this new frontier is just beginning. Let's explore it together.

CHAPTER 1: A BRIEF HISTORY OF ARTIFICIAL INTELLIGENCE

Artificial Intelligence (AI) has captured humanity's imagination for centuries, long before the advent of modern computing. From ancient myths of automatons to the groundbreaking technologies of the 21st century, the journey of AI is one of relentless curiosity, innovation, and discovery. This chapter takes you on a journey through the historical milestones that have defined AI, setting the stage for the transformative capabilities of GenAI explored in later chapters.

Rick Abbott
The Roots of AI: Dreams and Ideas

The concept of intelligent machines is as old as civilization itself. Ancient Greek myths, such as the story of Talos—a giant, bronze automaton—and the mechanical bird created by the Greek engineer Hero of Alexandria, showcase humanity's fascination with artificial life. These early imaginings laid the groundwork for the philosophical debates that would later shape the field of AI.

In the 17th century, philosophers like René Descartes and Thomas Hobbes began to explore the idea of mechanistic intelligence. Hobbes proposed that reasoning was nothing more than "computing," an idea that foreshadowed the development of modern computers. Later, the invention of programmable machines, such as Charles Babbage's Analytical Engine in the 19th century, brought humanity closer to realizing the dream of artificial intelligence.

The Dawn of Computing: Setting the Stage for AI

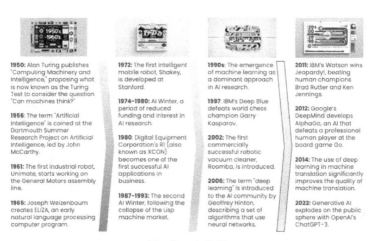

1950: Alan Turing publishes "Computing Machinery and Intelligence," proposing what is now known as the Turing Test to consider the question "Can machines think?"

1956: The term "Artificial Intelligence" is coined at the Dartmouth Summer Research Project on Artificial Intelligence, led by John McCarthy.

1961: The first industrial robot, Unimate, starts working on the General Motors assembly line.

1966: Joseph Weizenbaum creates ELIZA, an early natural language processing computer program.

1972: The first intelligent mobile robot, Shakey, is developed at Stanford.

1974-1980: AI Winter, a period of reduced funding and interest in AI research.

1980: Digital Equipment Corporation's R1 (also known as XCON) becomes one of the first successful AI applications in business.

1987-1993: The second AI Winter, following the collapse of the Lisp machine market.

1990s: The emergence of machine learning as a dominant approach in AI research.

1997: IBM's Deep Blue defeats world chess champion Garry Kasparov.

2002: The first commercially successful robotic vacuum cleaner, Roomba, is introduced.

2006: The term "deep learning" is introduced to the AI community by Geoffrey Hinton, describing a set of algorithms that use neural networks.

2011: IBM's Watson wins Jeopardy!, beating human champions Brad Rutter and Ken Jennings.

2012: Google's DeepMind develops AlphaGo, an AI that defeats a professional human player at the board game Go.

2014: The use of deep learning in machine translation significantly improves the quality of machine translation.

2022: Generative AI explodes on the public sphere with OpenAI's ChatGPT-3.

Timeline of AI Events

The 20th century marked a turning point for AI with the advent of digital computing. Alan Turing, often regarded as the father of computer science, made significant contributions to the field with his 1936 paper "On Computable Numbers," which introduced the concept of a universal machine capable of performing any computation. Turing's work laid the theoretical foundation for the programmable computers that would become essential for AI research.

During World War II, Turing further demonstrated the power of computing by developing machines to break the German Enigma code. This period of innovation highlighted the potential for machines to perform tasks that were previously thought to require human intelligence.

In 1950, Turing introduced the famous "Turing Test" as a measure of a machine's ability to exhibit intelligent behavior indistinguishable from that of a human. The Turing Test remains a benchmark in AI research, sparking debates about the nature of intelligence and consciousness.

The Birth of AI: The 1950s and 1960s

The term "artificial intelligence" was coined in 1956 at the Dartmouth Conference, organized by John McCarthy, Marvin Minsky, Nathaniel Rochester, and Claude Shannon. This seminal event marked the official beginning of AI as a field of study. Researchers at the conference envisioned a future where machines could reason, learn, and solve complex problems.

Early AI research focused on symbolic reasoning and rule-based systems. Programs like Logic Theorist, developed by Allen Newell and Herbert Simon, demonstrated the potential of machines to solve mathematical problems. These systems relied on formal logic and symbolic representation, laying the groundwork for future advancements.

During this period, optimism about AI's potential ran high. Researchers believed that machines capable of human-like reasoning were just around the corner. However, these early systems were limited by the computational power of the time and the complexity of real-world problems.

The AI Winters: Challenges and Setbacks

The 1970s and 1980s saw periods of stagnation in AI research, known as "AI winters." Funding and interest in AI waned as researchers encountered significant challenges. Early systems struggled with ambiguity, incomplete data, and the computational limitations of the era. Critics argued that AI's promises were overhyped, leading to skepticism and reduced investment.

Despite these setbacks, important progress was made during this time. The development of expert systems, which encoded domain-specific knowledge into rule-based systems, demonstrated practical applications of AI in fields like medicine and engineering. However, these systems were brittle and lacked the adaptability of human intelligence.

The Machine Learning Revolution: 1990s and 2000s

The resurgence of AI in the 1990s was driven by advances in machine learning, a subset of AI focused on training systems to learn from data. The proliferation of data and improvements in computational power enabled the development of more robust algorithms. Techniques like neural networks, which had been largely abandoned during the AI winters, experienced a revival with the advent of deep learning.

Landmark achievements during this period include IBM's Deep Blue defeating chess grandmaster Garry Kasparov in 1997 and the development of natural language processing (NLP) systems capable of understanding and generating human-like text. These milestones demonstrated the potential of AI to tackle complex, real-world problems.

The Age of GenAI: The 2010s and Beyond

The 2010s marked the emergence of GenAI, fueled by breakthroughs in deep learning and the availability of massive datasets. Generative models like Generative Adversarial Networks (GANs) and Variational Autoencoders (VAEs) enabled machines to create realistic images, videos, and audio. In parallel, large-scale language models like OpenAI's GPT series revolutionized natural language processing.

GenAI has since permeated various industries, from entertainment and healthcare to finance and retail. Its ability to generate creative and contextually relevant content has unlocked new possibilities for businesses and individuals alike. However, it has also raised important questions about ethics, bias, and the societal impact of AI-generated content.

Lessons from the Past

The history of AI is a story of ambition, resilience, and adaptation. Each era has brought new challenges and opportunities, shaping the field into what it is today. The journey from ancient myths to GenAI underscores the importance of collaboration between disciplines, including computer science, philosophy, psychology, and ethics.

As we delve deeper into the capabilities and implications of GenAI, it is essential to reflect on the lessons of the past. The successes and failures of earlier AI systems remind us that progress is neither linear nor guaranteed. By building on the foundations laid by generations of researchers and innovators, we can navigate the complexities of this new frontier with wisdom and foresight.

In the chapters ahead, we will explore how businesses can harness the power of GenAI to drive innovation and growth while addressing the ethical and practical challenges it presents. The history of AI is still being written, and you can shape its next chapter.

Key Takeaways

1. **The Origins of AI:** The idea of artificial intelligence has ancient roots, with early concepts appearing in mythology, philosophy, and early mechanical inventions.
2. **Turing's Legacy:** Alan Turing's work in computing and the Turing Test laid the theoretical and philosophical groundwork for AI as a scientific discipline.
3. **AI's Official Birth:** The Dartmouth Conference in 1956 marked the formal beginning of AI research, setting ambitious goals for machine reasoning and learning.
4. **Lessons from AI Winters:** Periods of stagnation in AI research highlight the importance of realistic expectations and the need for technological and computational advances.
5. **The GenAI Era:** Advances in deep learning and data availability have ushered in a new era of AI, characterized by creative and transformative applications across industries.

CHAPTER 2: INTRODUCTION TO GENERATIVE AI

GenAI represents a transformative subset of AI technologies designed to create new content across multiple mediums, including text, images, code, speech, synthetic data, and video among others. By leveraging advanced machine learning models—particularly deep learning networks—GenAI generates outputs that emulate the style, tone, and complexity of the input data it is trained on. Unlike traditional AI, which primarily focuses on tasks like prediction or classification, GenAI excels in producing creative and human-like outputs, offering unprecedented opportunities for innovation.

The Evolution of GenAI

GenAI's journey began with simple content-generation tools, evolving into sophisticated systems capable of producing highly nuanced and contextually relevant outputs. Early developments in text and image generation paved the way for advanced models such as GPT (Generative Pre-trained Transformer), Grok, Gemini, and DALL-E. Soon, the introduction of cutting-edge platforms like Sora is expected to further revolutionize this space. These advancements have fundamentally redefined how machines can understand and generate human-like content.

This technological evolution has been powered by breakthroughs in neural networks, the availability of vast datasets, and significant advancements in computing power. Together, these elements have enabled GenAI to move beyond basic functionality and into a realm where it can rival human creativity in many domains.

The Role of GenAI in Business

GenAI has quickly become a cornerstone for driving innovation across various business functions and industries. Its applications are as diverse as they are impactful, streamlining processes, enhancing customer engagement, and opening new avenues for growth.

Examples of business functions benefiting from GenAI include:

- **Marketing and Advertising**: GenAI creates personalized campaigns, compelling advertisements, and engaging content tailored to specific audiences. By analyzing consumer behavior, it helps marketers craft strategies that resonate with their target demographics.
- **Product Development**: From ideation to prototyping, GenAI accelerates the product design process by generating innovative concepts and simulating potential outcomes.
- **Customer Service**: AI-driven chatbots and virtual assistants provide personalized, 24/7 customer support, improving satisfaction and reducing operational costs.
- **Software Development**: GenAI automates code generation, debugging, and testing, significantly reducing development time and enhancing software quality.
- **Operations and Supply Chain**: By predicting demand and identifying inefficiencies, GenAI optimizes supply chain management and streamlines operations.

GenAI Capabilities

GenAI's versatility stems from its ability to produce diverse forms of digital content. Some of its most notable capabilities include:

- **Text Generation**: Producing written content such as articles, reports, stories, and even poetry. GenAI models can also convert text prompts into images, a capability known as text-to-image (T2I).
- **Image Creation**: Generating realistic or abstract images based on textual descriptions or modifying existing visuals.
- **Audio and Music Production**: Creating voiceovers, sound effects, and even complete musical compositions.
- **Video Synthesis**: Crafting original video content or editing existing footage with precision and creativity.
- **Voice and Speech Generation**: GenAI can now produce human-like speech, enabling applications in virtual assistants, audiobooks, and more. This includes the ability to modify voices and generate novel sounds, expanding creative possibilities in music and entertainment.
- **Code Development**: Automating the generation and debugging of code snippets, accelerating software development cycles.
- **Multimodal Functionality**: Advanced GenAI models can process and generate multiple types of data simultaneously, such as text, images, and audio. This enables more integrated and versatile applications, including creating content that combines various media forms.
- **Enhanced Reasoning and Problem-Solving**: Recent models focus on improved reasoning abilities, allowing them to tackle complex tasks that require step-by-step logical processes, such as advanced mathematics and coding challenges.
- **Real-Time Data Analysis and Decision-Making**: With advancements in processing power, GenAI systems can analyze data and make decisions in real time, enhancing applications in areas like autonomous vehicles and dynamic content creation.

These capabilities are underpinned by sophisticated technologies, including Generative Adversarial Networks (GANs), Large Language Models (LLMs), and advanced neural networks. Together, they enable

GenAI to mimic and enhance human creativity across multiple domains.

Ethical Considerations and Challenges

As with any transformative technology, the adoption of GenAI comes with significant ethical implications and challenges that organizations must address to ensure responsible and sustainable implementation. While GenAI offers transformative potential, its development and deployment require organizations to remain vigilant about unintended consequences that may arise. Addressing these ethical considerations not only minimizes risks but also fosters trust among stakeholders, employees, and customers, ensuring the long-term success of GenAI initiatives.

Key concerns include:

- **Bias in AI Models:** The training data used to develop GenAI models may inadvertently introduce biases, resulting in unfair or discriminatory outcomes. For example, if a model is trained on historically skewed data, it might reinforce stereotypes or overlook underrepresented groups in hiring, marketing, or other decision-making processes.
- **Data Privacy:** The use of vast amounts of data to train and operate GenAI raises concerns about compliance with data protection regulations such as GDPR, CCPA, and others. Organizations must ensure that customer data is handled securely and transparently to maintain trust and avoid legal repercussions.
- **Regulatory Compliance:** The fast-paced evolution of AI regulations globally requires organizations to stay informed and adapt quickly to new laws and standards. Non-compliance can result in hefty fines, reputational damage, and barriers to future innovation.
- **Transparency and Explainability:** One of the key challenges with GenAI systems, especially advanced models like neural networks, is their "black-box" nature, making it difficult to explain how decisions are made. Lack of transparency can lead to mistrust and make it challenging to address errors or biases.
- **Job Displacement Concerns:** The automation capabilities of GenAI, while enhancing efficiency, may lead to fears of job displacement among employees, potentially resulting in resistance to adoption and a negative organizational culture.

To address these challenges, businesses should implement robust data governance practices, regularly audit AI systems, and establish clear ethical guidelines. By proactively addressing these ethical concerns, organizations can mitigate risks while fully unlocking the transformative potential of GenAI. We will delve more deeply into the ethical and legal challenges related to GenAI in a later chapter.

Conclusion

GenAI is not merely a technological innovation; it is a strategic enabler for businesses seeking to thrive in an increasingly digital world. By automating complex tasks, enhancing creativity, and enabling data-driven decision-making, GenAI empowers organizations to achieve new levels of efficiency and innovation. However, its adoption must be guided by ethical principles and a commitment to responsible AI practices.

As businesses continue to explore the possibilities of GenAI, they must remain agile and informed, ready to adapt to the opportunities and challenges of this evolving technology.

Key Takeaways

1. **Creative Power of GenAI:** GenAI leverages advanced machine learning models to produce innovative and human-like content across text, images, audio, video, and code.
2. **Business Applications:** GenAI enhances marketing, customer service, product development, operational efficiency among many others, driving innovation across industries.
3. **Technological Foundations:** Key technologies like GANs, LLMs, and neural networks enable GenAI to mimic human creativity and generate contextually relevant outputs.
4. **Ethical Challenges:** Businesses must address potential biases, data privacy concerns, and evolving regulations to adopt GenAI responsibly.
5. **Transformative Potential:** By automating tasks and enabling new opportunities, GenAI empowers organizations to achieve efficiency, innovation, and competitive differentiation.

CHAPTER 3: ETHICAL, LEGAL, AND REGULATORY CONSIDERATIONS

Introduction

Before implementing GenAI in any organization, it is critical to address the ethical, legal, and regulatory considerations that underpin its responsible and effective use. Without a structured approach to these dimensions, organizations risk facing reputational, operational, and legal challenges that could undermine their AI initiatives. This chapter provides an overview of these three key areas, offering guidance to navigate the complexities of deploying GenAI responsibly.

The ethical deployment of GenAI involves addressing issues like bias, fairness, transparency, and accountability. GenAI systems are trained on vast datasets that may inadvertently reflect societal biases, leading to unfair or discriminatory outcomes. Mitigating these risks requires diverse and representative data, rigorous testing, and continuous monitoring to ensure outputs align with ethical standards. Transparency, interpretability, and explainability are vital to building trust. Organizations must make AI decision-making processes understandable, ensuring users can comprehend how and why decisions are made. Establishing clear accountability mechanisms and ethical governance frameworks helps guide AI use in alignment with societal values and fosters trust among stakeholders.

Legal considerations for GenAI focus on data privacy, intellectual property, and liability. Adhering to data protection regulations, such as Health Insurance Portability and Accountability Act (HIPAA), European Union's General Data Protection Regulation (GDPR), and the California Consumer Privacy Act (CCPA), is paramount to safeguarding sensitive personal information. Organizations must also navigate the complexities of intellectual property rights, particularly when GenAI systems generate new content or utilize copyrighted material during training. Liability frameworks are essential for assigning responsibility in cases where AI outputs cause harm or errors. By establishing clear legal policies and processes, organizations can reduce risks and ensure compliance with evolving regulations.

Regulatory frameworks for GenAI are rapidly evolving to address the unique challenges posed by this transformative technology. Governments and regulatory bodies are introducing guidelines and standards to promote transparency, accountability, and fairness in AI deployment. These frameworks, such as the European Union's proposed AI Act an the United States proposed Algorithmic Accountability Act of 2022, aim to balance innovation with societal safeguards. Organizations must proactively engage with these regulations, conduct regular compliance audits, and stay informed about changes to ensure adherence. Developing internal oversight mechanisms and collaborating with industry consortia can further help navigate the regulatory landscape.

By considering ethical, legal, and regulatory factors, organizations can implement GenAI responsibly, fostering trust, minimizing risks, and maximizing its transformative potential.

Ethical Considerations

Ethical considerations are a cornerstone of deploying GenAI responsibly, as the transformative power of this technology comes with complex risks and responsibilities. A key challenge lies in addressing bias and fairness within AI systems. GenAI models learn from vast datasets, which often reflect historical inequities or societal biases. These embedded biases can result in outputs that perpetuate discrimination or unfair treatment, especially in sensitive applications like hiring, lending, or content generation. Ensuring fairness requires organizations to use diverse and representative datasets, rigorously test and validate AI models, and continuously monitor their performance to detect and mitigate biases. These efforts are essential to creating systems that deliver equitable and reliable results.

Transparency and explainability are equally critical when implementing GenAI. These systems are often described as "black boxes" due to the complexity of their underlying algorithms, which can obscure how decisions are made. This lack of transparency can erode trust among users and stakeholders, making it challenging to hold the system accountable for its outputs. To address this, organizations must focus on improving the interpretability of GenAI systems by developing tools that make their decision-making processes understandable. Clear communication about the system's purpose, limitations, and rationale for decisions fosters trust and empowers stakeholders to engage with AI systems confidently.

Accountability is another crucial aspect of ethical AI deployment. When GenAI systems fail or cause harm, determining who is responsible—the developers, the organization deploying the AI, or other parties—can become a contentious issue. To ensure accountability, organizations need to establish clear protocols for oversight and intervention, define roles and responsibilities for managing AI systems, and set up ethics committees or review boards to provide ongoing governance. These measures help create a framework where negative outcomes can be addressed systematically, and responsibility is clearly assigned.

Privacy and data protection are fundamental ethical concerns, as GenAI systems rely heavily on large datasets that often include sensitive information. Safeguarding this data from breaches and unauthorized access is essential to maintaining trust and complying with regulations such as GDPR and CCPA. Robust data anonymization techniques, secure storage practices, and adherence to data protection laws are critical steps in mitigating privacy risks. By proactively addressing these ethical challenges, organizations can ensure that their GenAI deployments are aligned with societal values, fostering trust and acceptance while unlocking the technology's full potential.

Legal Implications

Deploying GenAI within a business setting necessitates attention to legal implications, foremost among them being compliance with data protection laws such as HIPPA, GDPR, and the CCPA. These regulations mandate stringent controls over the collection, storage, and processing of personal data. Organizations must ensure that they collect, store, and use data in accordance with these regulations, which may include obtaining informed consent from data subjects, anonymizing or pseudonymizing data where possible, and implementing robust security measures to protect against data breaches. Non-compliance can result in hefty fines and damage to a company's reputation.

Another critical legal aspect is intellectual property rights. GenAI systems often create new content, raising questions about the ownership of these creations. Businesses must navigate the complexities of intellectual property law to determine who holds the rights to AI-generated works. Using copyrighted material to train AI models without proper authorization can lead to legal disputes. Establishing clear policies on the use of data and respecting intellectual property rights is essential to mitigate legal risks.

Employment law and workforce impacts are also significant considerations. GenAI can automate tasks previously performed by humans, leading to job displacement and changes in workforce dynamics. Companies must adhere to employment laws regarding layoffs, retraining, and fair labor practices. They should also consider the ethical implications of workforce reductions and invest in reskilling programs to support employees transitioning to new roles within the organization.

Liability and risk management are crucial in the deployment of GenAI. Determining liability when AI systems malfunction or cause harm can be challenging. Businesses must establish clear liability frameworks that delineate responsibility between AI developers, users, and third-party vendors. Implementing comprehensive risk management strategies, including regular audits, impact assessments, and having contingency plans in place, can help mitigate potential legal issues.

Regulatory Frameworks

The current regulatory landscape for GenAI is evolving rapidly, reflecting the growing importance and complexity of AI technologies. Various jurisdictions have introduced or are developing regulations to address the unique challenges posed by GenAI. These regulations aim to ensure that AI is developed and deployed in ways that are ethical, transparent, and beneficial to society. Notable examples include the European Union's AI Act, which seeks to establish comprehensive rules for AI applications, and previously mentioned data protection regulations like HIPPA, GDPR, and CCPA that govern the use of personal data by AI systems. Also active are the European Commission, the U.S. Federal Trade Commission, and the U.K. Information Commissioner's Office, which work to establish guidelines and standards for the development and deployment of GenAI technologies.

The role of regulatory bodies is crucial in shaping and enforcing these frameworks. These bodies are responsible for developing guidelines, conducting audits, and imposing sanctions on entities that fail to comply with regulatory requirements. Their efforts help maintain a balance between fostering innovation and protecting public interests.

Key regulations affecting GenAI deployment encompass various issues, from data protection and privacy to ethical use and accountability. The GDPR and CCPA impose stringent requirements on how businesses collect, store, and process personal data. The proposed EU AI Act classifies AI systems based on risk levels and imposes specific obligations accordingly, such as conducting impact assessments and ensuring transparency. Sector-specific regulations may apply, such as those governing healthcare, finance, and autonomous vehicles, each adding another layer of compliance for businesses deploying GenAI.

To navigate this complex regulatory environment, businesses must adopt best practices for compliance. This includes conducting regular compliance audits, implementing robust data governance frameworks, and ensuring transparency in AI decision-making processes. Developing a comprehensive AI ethics policy and establishing internal review boards can also help preemptively address potential regulatory issues. Engaging with regulatory bodies and participating in industry consortia can inform businesses about regulatory changes and emerging best practices.

Future directions in AI regulation will likely focus on enhancing transparency, accountability, and ethical considerations in AI deployment. As AI technologies evolve, regulatory frameworks must adapt to address new challenges, such as the ethical use of AI in decision-making, the mitigation of algorithmic biases, and the protection of individual rights in the face of increasing automation. Collaborative efforts between regulators, industry stakeholders, and civil society will be essential to create regulations that promote innovation while safeguarding public trust and safety.

Building a GenAI Governance Framework

Building a robust GenAI governance framework is essential for ensuring the ethical, legal, and effective deployment of GenAI within an organization. A crucial first step is establishing a cross-functional AI Program Management Office (AI PMO). This AI PMO should include representatives from various departments such as IT, legal, HR, compliance, and business units to ensure a holistic approach to AI governance. This diversity helps address the multifaceted challenges posed by AI, from technical issues to ethical dilemmas and regulatory compliance. The AI PMO's role includes overseeing GenAI projects, aligning them with organizational goals, and ensuring all stakeholders are informed and engaged throughout the implementation process. It should also identify and mitigate potential risks of GenAI, such as data privacy, security, and bias. Organizations can ensure that GenAI is implemented to align with their overall business objectives and ethical standards by establishing clear roles and responsibilities within the AI PMO.

Developing comprehensive policies and procedures for GenAI use is another critical component of the governance framework. These policies should cover all aspects of AI deployment, including data privacy, ethical use, transparency, and accountability. Clear guidelines must be established on how data is collected, processed, and utilized by GenAI systems. Procedures should define the responsibilities of different teams and outline the steps for risk management and incident response. Effective policies ensure that AI initiatives comply with legal standards and align with the organization's ethical values. Organizations should develop policies for algorithm development and model deployment to prevent the introduction of biases and ensure that GenAI systems are transparent and explainable. This includes establishing processes for validating and monitoring AI models to ensure they perform as intended and do not produce harmful or misleading outputs.

Monitoring and auditing GenAI systems for compliance is essential to maintain trust and reliability in AI deployments. Regular audits should be conducted to evaluate AI models' performance, fairness, and transparency. This involves setting up mechanisms to detect and mitigate biases, ensuring that AI decisions are explainable, and verifying that all operations comply with the established policies and legal requirements. Continuous monitoring helps identify potential issues early and enables timely corrective actions. It also provides an ongoing assessment of the AI systems' impact on the organization and its stakeholders, fostering a culture of continuous improvement and accountability. Auditing should be conducted by an independent body to maintain objectivity and ensure the integrity of the process. The results of these audits should be used to identify areas for improvement and inform updates to the GenAI governance framework. By continuously monitoring and auditing GenAI systems, organizations can demonstrate their commitment to responsible AI use and maintain the trust of their users and stakeholders.

By integrating these elements—establishing a cross-functional AI PMO, developing robust policies and procedures, and ensuring rigorous monitoring and auditing—organizations can build a comprehensive GenAI governance framework. This framework mitigates risks and maximizes AI's benefits, ensuring its ethical and effective deployment in alignment with organizational values and regulatory standards.

Case Studies

Examining case studies of legal challenges in GenAI deployments provides valuable insights into the complexities of navigating these legal waters. Legal disputes have arisen over biased AI decision-making in hiring processes and issues related to the unauthorized use of data. Learning from these cases can guide businesses in developing robust legal and ethical frameworks to avoid similar pitfalls. By proactively addressing legal implications, companies can foster a responsible and legally compliant approach to deploying GenAI.

Several legal challenges have already arisen in the context of GenAI deployments. For example, in 2020, the Authors Guild filed a lawsuit against OpenAI, the GPT-3 language model developer, alleging copyright infringement. The lawsuit claimed that OpenAI's use of copyrighted material in training its AI models amounted to unauthorized copying and violated authors' rights. This case highlights the importance of considering intellectual property rights when deploying GenAI technologies.

In another case, a group of artists filed a lawsuit against several AI companies, alleging that their AI systems were being used to generate images that infringed on the artists' copyrights. The artists argued that the AI systems were trained on their copyrighted works without permission and that the resulting images constituted unauthorized derivative works. This case underscores the need for organizations to carefully consider the legal implications of using GenAI for content creation.

Best Practices from Leading Companies:

Leading companies are adopting best practices to maximize the potential of GenAI while addressing its unique challenges. One key strategy is customizing GenAI tools to meet industry-specific needs. By tailoring machine learning algorithms and datasets to the specific demands and regulations of their industries, organizations can enhance the accuracy, reliability, and effectiveness of their AI solutions. This approach ensures that GenAI applications are not only optimized for their intended use but also comply with relevant industry standards and regulatory requirements.

Another critical practice is fostering a culture of curiosity and continuous learning. To fully leverage GenAI's capabilities, organizations must stay informed about the latest developments, proactively identify potential challenges, and invest in the necessary resources to deepen their understanding of GenAI tools and applications. This culture of ongoing education and innovation enables companies to adapt quickly to technological advancements, address emerging issues, and unlock new opportunities for growth and efficiency.

Equally important is prioritizing human oversight and responsibility in GenAI deployments. Successful implementations emphasize the "human-in-the-loop" approach, ensuring that AI systems operate as collaborative tools rather than autonomous decision-makers. Organizations must establish a structured framework for monitoring and mitigating biases, providing clear guidelines for the ethical and responsible use of GenAI technologies. By combining technological innovation with human judgment and accountability, companies can ensure that GenAI is deployed in a way that aligns with their values and objectives while maintaining trust and fairness in its outcomes.

Conclusion

This chapter has addressed the critical ethical, legal, and regulatory considerations necessary for the responsible deployment of GenAI within businesses. We explored key areas such as bias and fairness in AI algorithms, transparency and explainability, privacy and data protection, accountability and responsibility, and the establishment of ethical governance frameworks. We examined the legal implications of GenAI, including compliance with data protection laws, intellectual property rights, employment law, and liability and risk management. Understanding these elements is crucial for organizations to navigate the complexities of GenAI and ensure its beneficial integration.

As AI technologies evolve, so do the ethical and legal challenges they present. Organizations must remain proactive in updating their policies and practices to reflect new developments in AI and regulations. Ethical vigilance involves continuous monitoring, regular audits, and a commitment to transparency and accountability. Legal vigilance requires staying informed about changes in legislation and ensuring that all AI-related activities comply with current laws. A culture of ethical and legal vigilance fosters trust and mitigates risks associated with AI deployment.

Businesses must establish comprehensive governance frameworks encompassing ethical guidelines, legal compliance, and robust monitoring systems. Companies should create cross-functional AI governance committees to oversee GenAI projects, develop clear policies and procedures, and implement regular audits to ensure compliance and accountability. By taking these steps, businesses can harness the power of GenAI while safeguarding against potential risks and ethical pitfalls.

Key Takeaways

1. **Addressing Bias and Ensuring Fairness:** AI models, including GenAI, often inherit biases from training data. Organizations must rigorously test and monitor AI systems, using diverse datasets to prevent discrimination and ensure equitable outcomes.
2. **Transparency, Interpretability, and Explainability:** Enhancing the transparency of GenAI systems by making decision-making processes understandable is crucial for

building trust. Explainable AI fosters accountability and facilitates stakeholder oversight.

3. **Data Privacy and Protection:** Safeguarding personal and sensitive data is essential. Adhering to data protection laws like HIPPQ and the CCPA, implementing secure data practices, and using anonymization techniques are critical for mitigating privacy risks.

4. **Ethical and Legal Governance Frameworks:** Establishing comprehensive governance frameworks with clear policies and cross-functional AI oversight ensures ethical and legal compliance. This includes creating guidelines for transparency, accountability, and risk management.

5. **Navigating Legal Complexities:** Compliance with data protection laws, intellectual property rights, and employment regulations is critical for GenAI deployment. Organizations must establish liability frameworks and implement proactive risk management to mitigate potential legal disputes.

CHAPTER 4: MANUFACTURING

Introduction to GenAI in Manufacturing

Manufacturing is the backbone of modern economies, driving technological innovation, economic growth, and job creation. It spans industries ranging from automotive and aerospace to consumer goods and electronics, producing the essential products that shape our everyday lives. As a critical pillar of global commerce, manufacturing also plays a pivotal role in supply chain integration, resource utilization, and economic resilience, making efficiency and innovation paramount for sustained competitiveness.

High-Level Explanation of GenAI's Relevance

GenAI is revolutionizing manufacturing by introducing transformative capabilities that enhance operational efficiency, reduce costs, and improve overall supply chain agility. Unlike traditional AI, which focuses primarily on predictive and analytical functions, GenAI excels in creating and synthesizing new solutions, ranging from optimized production schedules to AI-generated product designs. Its ability to analyze massive datasets, simulate complex processes, and make real-time adjustments enables manufacturers to tackle some of their most persistent challenges.

GenAI can streamline workflows by automating labor-intensive tasks like inventory management and quality control, while also generating actionable insights to enhance production line efficiency. By integrating GenAI into smart factories and supply chain networks, manufacturers can predict market demand, mitigate disruptions, and adapt to fluctuations with unparalleled precision. This capability not only drives profitability but also empowers businesses to meet evolving consumer expectations for customization, sustainability, and speed.

Current Challenges and Gaps in Manufacturing

The manufacturing industry faces a number of challenges that hinder its ability to operate at peak efficiency. Among these are inefficiencies in production planning, a lack of real-time visibility into supply chains, and rising costs due to labor shortages and material price volatility. These gaps have been exacerbated by the increasing complexity of global supply chains, where disruptions from natural disasters, geopolitical tensions, or pandemics can have cascading effects on production and delivery schedules.

Another persistent challenge is quality assurance, as traditional inspection methods often fail to detect defects until they have propagated through multiple stages of production. This not only leads to wasted resources but also damages brand reputation. Achieving sustainability goals remains a daunting task for manufacturers, as they struggle to balance operational demands with reducing energy consumption and minimizing waste.

GenAI addresses these gaps by offering predictive capabilities that foresee potential disruptions and inefficiencies before they occur. For instance, AI-powered quality assurance systems can detect minute defects in real time, ensuring higher product reliability while reducing costs associated with rework. GenAI-driven sustainability analytics provide actionable recommendations for resource optimization, helping manufacturers meet environmental standards without sacrificing productivity. By bridging these gaps, GenAI empowers the manufacturing sector to achieve unprecedented levels of efficiency, innovation, and adaptability.

Transformational Impact

GenAI is at the forefront of a new industrial revolution, redefining the manufacturing landscape through intelligent automation, real-time analytics, and innovative design capabilities. By integrating GenAI into smart factories, manufacturers are achieving operational efficiencies that were previously unimaginable. For example, GenAI-powered systems optimize production schedules by analyzing multiple variables—such as machine availability, labor allocation, and material supply—in real time, enabling manufacturers to maximize throughput while minimizing delays.

GenAI enhances product design by generating prototypes and optimizing components based on performance criteria, cost constraints, and sustainability goals. Tools like Generative Adversarial Networks (GANs) enable manufacturers to simulate various design scenarios and select the most effective solutions without extensive physical testing. This accelerates time-to-market for new products, giving businesses a critical edge in competitive markets.

In supply chain management, GenAI drives agility and resilience by providing real-time insights into logistics, inventory levels, and supplier performance. AI-powered systems can anticipate potential disruptions, such as delays in raw material deliveries, and recommend alternative suppliers or routes, ensuring continuity in production. These capabilities are transforming how manufacturers operate, allowing them to shift from reactive troubleshooting to proactive optimization.

Changes in Workflows and Decision-Making

The integration of GenAI into manufacturing processes is revolutionizing traditional workflows, replacing manual interventions with data-driven, automated solutions. Quality control processes that once relied on human inspection are now enhanced by GenAI-powered vision systems capable of identifying defects with far greater accuracy and speed. This automation not only reduces human error but also frees up workers to focus on higher-value tasks such as innovation and strategy.

Decision-making is also evolving, with GenAI providing actionable insights derived from large-scale data analysis. Production managers can now rely on AI-generated recommendations to make real-time decisions about resource allocation, equipment maintenance, and workforce deployment. This shift towards data-informed decision-making ensures precision, efficiency, and consistency across operations, enabling manufacturers to adapt quickly to changing demands.

The Shift in Focus Due to GenAI Adoption

The adoption of GenAI is shifting the focus of manufacturing priorities from cost-cutting and mass production to agility, customization, and sustainability. As consumer preferences for personalized products grow, manufacturers are leveraging GenAI to enable mass customization at scale. By integrating AI into production lines, businesses can seamlessly adjust processes to create bespoke products without sacrificing efficiency.

Sustainability has also emerged as a key priority. GenAI empowers manufacturers to monitor energy usage, reduce waste, and optimize material consumption, all while maintaining profitability. AI-driven sustainability analytics can identify energy-saving opportunities and recommend changes to manufacturing practices that minimize environmental impact. This alignment with global sustainability goals not only enhances brand reputation but also ensures compliance with increasingly stringent regulations.

Top Opportunities for GenAI in Manufacturing

GenAI unlocks numerous opportunities for the manufacturing sector to achieve meaningful impact. Key areas include:

- **AI-Driven Predictive Maintenance**: By analyzing sensor data from machinery, GenAI identifies signs of wear or potential failure, enabling proactive maintenance that minimizes downtime and extends equipment lifespan.
- **Intelligent Demand Forecasting**: GenAI predicts market demand with precision, allowing manufacturers to adjust production volumes and inventory levels to meet customer needs while avoiding overproduction.
- **Automated Quality Assurance**: AI-powered vision systems detect defects in real time, ensuring consistent product

quality and reducing costs associated with rework and returns.

- **Dynamic Supply Chain Resilience**: GenAI provides real-time insights into supply chain dynamics, enabling manufacturers to respond to disruptions quickly by identifying alternative suppliers, routes, or materials.
- **Sustainable Production Practices**: GenAI helps manufacturers optimize energy consumption, reduce material waste, and implement circular economy strategies, meeting both economic and environmental goals.

The transformative potential of GenAI in manufacturing is evident in its ability to enhance efficiency, foster innovation, and promote sustainability. By automating workflows, enabling real-time decision-making, and addressing critical challenges, GenAI empowers manufacturers to stay competitive in an increasingly dynamic market. This shift not only drives profitability but also positions manufacturing as a forward-looking industry capable of meeting the demands of a changing world.

Key Technologies and Tools

GenAI is revolutionizing manufacturing by introducing a suite of cutting-edge tools and technologies designed to enhance efficiency, streamline processes, and foster innovation. Among the most impactful tools are Generative Adversarial Networks (GANs), which are widely used for optimizing product designs and simulating various production scenarios. Predictive analytics platforms powered by advanced machine learning models enable precise demand forecasting and real-time quality assurance. AI-powered vision systems use convolutional neural networks (CNNs) to detect defects in manufacturing processes, ensuring higher reliability and lower waste. Tools like these provide manufacturers with the agility to adapt to dynamic market conditions and the precision to achieve operational excellence.

Platforms such as Microsoft Azure AI, Google Cloud AI, and IBM Watson are also central to integrating GenAI into manufacturing operations. These platforms offer end-to-end solutions for building, training, and deploying AI models, enabling businesses to scale their GenAI applications efficiently. By leveraging these technologies, manufacturers can unlock new levels of productivity and innovation, transforming traditional workflows into AI-powered ecosystems.

Integration with Existing Technologies

The successful adoption of GenAI in manufacturing depends on its seamless integration with existing systems and technologies. Manufacturing Execution Systems (MES) and Enterprise Resource Planning (ERP) platforms like SAP S/4HANA are critical for managing operations and supply chains. Integrating GenAI into these systems allows manufacturers to automate workflows, improve decision-making, and optimize resource allocation in real time.

GenAI can enhance MES platforms by providing predictive analytics for machine maintenance, reducing unexpected downtime. ERP systems integrated with GenAI tools can automate inventory management, ensuring optimal stock levels based on real-time demand forecasting. GenAI tools can be embedded in Supply Chain Management (SCM) systems to monitor supplier performance and identify risks, enabling proactive strategies to mitigate disruptions.

Interoperability is key to successful integration. By leveraging APIs and middleware, manufacturers can connect GenAI models to legacy systems, creating a unified data ecosystem that ensures accurate and consistent insights. Data standardization and governance frameworks further enhance integration efforts, enabling smoother workflows and more effective use of AI-driven insights. Cybersecurity measures, including encryption and access controls, are essential to safeguard sensitive data and maintain compliance with industry regulations.

Technical Trends Influencing Manufacturing

Several emerging trends are reshaping the manufacturing industry, driven by advancements in GenAI and related technologies. These trends are enabling manufacturers to enhance productivity, reduce waste, and achieve greater operational agility. Key trends include:

- **Digital Twins**: Digital twins create virtual replicas of physical assets, such as production lines or individual machines. By integrating GenAI, digital twins provide real-time insights into performance, allowing manufacturers to simulate scenarios, optimize processes, and prevent bottlenecks before they occur.
- **Hyper-Automation**: GenAI-powered automation extends beyond isolated tasks, enabling end-to-end workflows across manufacturing operations. By combining AI, robotics, and

IoT, hyper-automation minimizes manual intervention, improves accuracy, and accelerates production timelines.

- **Edge Computing**: As manufacturing processes demand real-time decision-making, edge computing enables GenAI to process data locally at the production site. This reduces latency, enhances responsiveness, and supports applications like predictive maintenance and dynamic quality control.
- **Sustainability Analytics**: With increasing pressure to adopt eco-friendly practices, GenAI supports sustainability initiatives by analyzing energy consumption, tracking material usage, and identifying opportunities to reduce waste. These insights help manufacturers meet environmental standards while maintaining profitability.
- **AI-Enabled Customization**: GenAI is transforming mass production into mass customization by enabling manufacturers to produce highly personalized products at scale. AI-driven tools analyze customer preferences and translate them into production specifications, ensuring efficient customization.

The integration of GenAI technologies into manufacturing is redefining how businesses operate, innovate, and compete. From digital twins that simulate real-time operations to sustainability analytics that drive eco-friendly practices, these technologies offer manufacturers the tools to stay ahead in an increasingly dynamic market. By adopting these key technologies and aligning them with industry trends, manufacturers can unlock unprecedented opportunities for growth, efficiency, and innovation.

Challenges and Risks

The integration of GenAI in manufacturing brings transformative benefits, but it also raises critical ethical concerns. One significant challenge is the potential displacement of workers as automation takes over tasks traditionally performed by humans. While GenAI enhances efficiency and reduces costs, it can lead to workforce reductions or changes in job roles, creating economic and social implications for affected employees. Manufacturers must balance technological advancement with their responsibility to support workforce transition through reskilling and upskilling initiatives.

Another ethical issue involves data privacy and security. GenAI systems rely heavily on large volumes of operational and supply chain data to function effectively. This data often includes sensitive information about suppliers, production processes, and customer preferences. Any misuse, unauthorized access, or breaches of this data can lead to significant reputational and financial damage. Manufacturers must implement robust data governance frameworks to protect privacy and ensure compliance with regulations such as GDPR and industry-specific standards.

Risks of Misuse or Over-Dependency

While GenAI offers remarkable capabilities, its misuse or over-dependency poses substantial risks. Over-reliance on AI systems for decision-making can lead to unintended consequences, particularly in complex or unforeseen scenarios where human judgment remains crucial. For instance, a manufacturing plant overly dependent on GenAI for production planning might struggle to adapt if the AI system produces inaccurate forecasts due to unexpected data anomalies.

GenAI systems may inadvertently introduce or perpetuate biases, especially in supplier evaluations or workforce management. If the training data for GenAI models is incomplete or biased, the resulting decisions could unfairly disadvantage certain suppliers or employees. This lack of transparency in AI-driven decisions, often referred to as the "black box" problem, makes it challenging to identify and rectify such biases.

Another risk involves the potential for operational vulnerabilities. Cyberattacks targeting GenAI systems could disrupt manufacturing processes, compromise sensitive data, or even manipulate AI-driven production schedules. This highlights the importance of prioritizing cybersecurity measures and maintaining contingency plans to ensure operational resilience.

Frameworks for Mitigating Risks

To address these challenges and risks, manufacturers must adopt proactive measures and establish robust frameworks to guide the ethical and effective use of GenAI. Key approaches include:

- **Workforce Reskilling Programs**: Implement comprehensive training programs to prepare employees for AI-driven roles. Equip workers with skills in AI tool operation, data analysis, and human-AI collaboration to ensure a smooth transition and retain workforce value.

- **Bias Audits and Validation**: Regularly audit GenAI models to detect and eliminate biases in their algorithms. Use diverse and representative datasets during model training to ensure fairness in AI-driven decisions.
- **Data Security Measures**: Establish stringent cybersecurity protocols, including encryption, access controls, and regular vulnerability assessments, to protect sensitive manufacturing and supply chain data from breaches and misuse.
- **Human-AI Collaboration Models**: Maintain a "human-in-the-loop" approach where critical decisions are reviewed by human experts, ensuring that AI recommendations align with organizational goals and values.
- **Regulatory Compliance Checks**: Regularly evaluate GenAI systems to ensure adherence to industry standards and regulations, such as those governing product safety, environmental impact, and data privacy.

The adoption of GenAI in manufacturing is not without its challenges, but with careful planning and ethical considerations, these risks can be effectively managed. By investing in workforce development, ensuring robust data governance, and fostering collaboration between humans and AI, manufacturers can harness GenAI's transformative potential while mitigating its risks. These strategies not only build trust among stakeholders but also position manufacturers as responsible leaders in the AI-driven industrial era.

Skillset Evolution

The introduction of GenAI into manufacturing is reshaping the skills required for professionals at every level. Traditional roles focused on manual tasks and routine decision-making are evolving into positions that demand technical expertise, data-driven insights, and a deep understanding of AI systems. For instance, production managers now need to interpret AI-generated analytics to optimize workflows, while engineers must integrate GenAI tools into existing machinery and processes. The ability to collaborate effectively with AI systems and leverage their capabilities is becoming a critical competency in modern manufacturing.

Professionals must also develop a strong foundation in AI literacy, including understanding how GenAI models work, their limitations, and the ethical considerations associated with their use. Soft skills such as problem-solving, adaptability, and cross-functional collaboration are equally vital, enabling workers to bridge the gap between human intuition and AI precision. As manufacturing continues to embrace digital transformation, the workforce must adapt to thrive in this AI-enhanced environment.

Training and Upskilling Needs

To prepare for the widespread adoption of GenAI, manufacturers must invest in targeted training and upskilling initiatives. Training programs should focus on equipping employees with the knowledge and technical skills needed to operate and manage AI-driven systems. Key areas of focus include:

- **AI Literacy**: Provide foundational training in AI concepts, such as machine learning, neural networks, and data analytics. This ensures employees understand the principles underlying GenAI technologies and their applications in manufacturing.
- **Tool Proficiency**: Offer hands-on training with GenAI-powered platforms and tools, such as predictive maintenance software, digital twins, and AI-enhanced quality control systems. Employees should gain practical experience in deploying and optimizing these technologies.
- **Data Analytics and Interpretation**: Teach employees how to analyze and interpret data generated by GenAI systems. This includes identifying actionable insights, validating AI outputs, and using these findings to make informed decisions.
- **Change Management**: Equip teams with skills to navigate organizational shifts associated with GenAI integration. Training should emphasize adaptability, teamwork, and communication to foster a culture of collaboration and innovation.

Upskilling efforts must also address leadership development, ensuring that managers and executives are prepared to guide teams through the transition to AI-driven manufacturing. Leadership training should focus on strategic planning, ethical considerations, and the integration of AI insights into broader business goals.

Emerging Roles in Manufacturing

As GenAI becomes integral to manufacturing, new roles are emerging to meet the demands of this technology-driven landscape. These roles combine technical expertise with operational knowledge, creating opportunities for professionals to specialize in AI applications within manufacturing. Key emerging roles include:

- **AI Operations Engineer**: Responsible for implementing and maintaining AI-driven systems on the production floor. This role involves configuring GenAI tools, optimizing workflows, and troubleshooting technical issues to ensure seamless integration.
- **Predictive Maintenance Analyst**: Leverages GenAI-powered analytics to monitor machinery health, identify potential failures, and schedule proactive maintenance. This role minimizes downtime and extends equipment lifespan.
- **Sustainability Data Specialist**: Uses AI tools to track energy consumption, material usage, and waste generation. This role focuses on optimizing production processes to meet sustainability goals while maintaining cost efficiency.
- **Human-AI Workflow Coordinator**: Acts as a bridge between AI systems and human teams, ensuring effective collaboration and communication. This role emphasizes the complementary strengths of human creativity and AI precision.
- **Supply Chain AI Strategist**: Develops and implements GenAI-driven strategies to enhance supply chain visibility, resilience, and efficiency. This role focuses on leveraging AI insights to optimize logistics, supplier relationships, and inventory management.

The adoption of GenAI in manufacturing is transforming the workforce, requiring a shift in skills, mindsets, and roles. By investing in comprehensive training programs and fostering a culture of continuous learning, manufacturers can empower their employees to excel in an AI-driven environment. These efforts not only prepare the workforce for the future but also position manufacturing organizations to capitalize on the full potential of GenAI, ensuring sustained innovation, competitiveness, and growth.

Emerging Trends

GenAI is poised to reshape the manufacturing landscape, driving a paradigm shift toward smarter, more sustainable, and highly adaptable operations. GenAI's integration will enable fully autonomous factories, where AI systems manage end-to-end production with minimal human intervention. These "lights-out" facilities will rely on GenAI for predictive maintenance, dynamic resource allocation, and real-time quality assurance, ensuring unparalleled efficiency and precision. As global supply chains grow increasingly complex, GenAI will play a pivotal role in fostering resilience, offering manufacturers the agility to navigate disruptions and evolving market demands with ease.

Emerging Trends and Their Potential Influence

Several transformative trends are accelerating GenAI's adoption in manufacturing, offering significant opportunities for innovation and growth:

- **Zero-Waste Manufacturing**: GenAI is driving the transition toward zero-waste production models by analyzing material usage, identifying inefficiencies, and recommending sustainable alternatives. Manufacturers are leveraging AI to reduce scrap rates, recycle by-products, and optimize energy consumption, aligning operations with environmental goals.
- **On-Demand Production Models**: The rise of mass customization is pushing manufacturers to adopt on-demand production enabled by GenAI. AI-driven systems adjust workflows in real time to accommodate unique customer specifications, minimizing inventory costs and accelerating delivery times while meeting the demand for personalized products.
- **Global AI-Oriented Ecosystems**: As manufacturers adopt GenAI, the industry is moving toward interconnected, AI-powered ecosystems. These networks use shared data and AI insights to optimize collaboration between suppliers, manufacturers, and distributors, improving efficiency and reducing costs across the value chain.
- **Digital Workforce Integration**: The integration of AI-powered tools into the manufacturing workforce is augmenting human capabilities rather than replacing them. GenAI is enabling workers to focus on strategic decision-making, creativity, and innovation while automating repetitive or hazardous tasks.
- **Resilience through Real-Time Data**: GenAI's ability to process vast amounts of real-time data is transforming how manufacturers respond to disruptions. AI systems monitor supply chains, detect potential issues, and recommend proactive solutions, ensuring continuity in production even during global crises or sudden demand shifts.

Strategic Priorities for Organizations

To fully capitalize on these trends, manufacturers must adopt forward-thinking strategies that align with GenAI's capabilities. Key strategic priorities include:

- **Investing in AI-Driven Sustainability Initiatives**: Commit resources to integrate GenAI tools that optimize resource utilization, track carbon footprints, and identify energy-saving opportunities. These efforts not only reduce environmental impact but also enhance brand reputation and compliance with regulations.
- **Scaling Adaptive Manufacturing Models**: Develop scalable systems that leverage GenAI to support flexible production lines capable of adapting to market changes. This includes integrating AI into robotics, additive manufacturing, and agile supply chain networks.
- **Building Data-Centric Ecosystems**: Create interconnected platforms that facilitate real-time data sharing across stakeholders. Implementing GenAI-driven dashboards and predictive analytics tools ensures informed decision-making and fosters seamless collaboration.
- **Empowering the Workforce for AI Collaboration**: Focus on reskilling initiatives to prepare employees for AI-enhanced roles. Promote a culture of innovation and adaptability, encouraging workers to experiment with GenAI technologies and drive creative problem-solving.
- **Implementing Ethical AI Governance Frameworks**: Establish clear policies to ensure responsible use of GenAI, addressing concerns around data privacy, algorithmic fairness, and transparency. Regular audits and compliance checks build trust among stakeholders and mitigate risks.

The convergence of GenAI and manufacturing is creating unprecedented opportunities for innovation, efficiency, and resilience. By aligning their strategies with emerging trends, manufacturers can unlock the full potential of GenAI, driving transformative growth while addressing societal demands for sustainability and customization. Those who adapt proactively to these changes will not only gain a competitive edge but also shape the future of manufacturing in the AI era.

Conclusion

GenAI is revolutionizing the manufacturing industry by enhancing efficiency, reducing costs, and driving innovation across operations and supply chains. From predictive maintenance and automated quality assurance to on-demand production and sustainability initiatives, GenAI is empowering manufacturers to overcome longstanding challenges and seize new opportunities. This technology is enabling real-time decision-making, fostering adaptability, and positioning manufacturing organizations to thrive in an era defined by rapid technological advancements and dynamic consumer demands.

Strategic Thinking and Adaptability

To fully harness the transformative power of GenAI, manufacturers must approach its adoption with strategic foresight and adaptability. Successful implementation requires aligning AI initiatives with organizational goals, such as improving production efficiency, enhancing customer satisfaction, and achieving sustainability targets. Integrating GenAI into existing systems and workflows must be done thoughtfully, ensuring that the technology complements and enhances human expertise rather than replacing it.

Equally critical is fostering a culture of innovation and continuous improvement. As GenAI evolves, so too will its applications in manufacturing. Organizations must remain agile, ready to embrace emerging trends and refine their strategies to address shifting market conditions. By investing in upskilling programs, manufacturers can prepare their workforce to collaborate effectively with AI systems, bridging the gap between technological advancements and operational excellence.

The Path Forward

The journey to GenAI-driven manufacturing is not without its challenges, including ethical considerations, workforce transformation, and operational risks. However, with robust governance frameworks, proactive risk mitigation, and a commitment to ethical practices, manufacturers can navigate these complexities successfully. Emphasizing transparency, data security, and fairness will build trust among stakeholders and ensure the responsible use of AI technologies.

As manufacturing organizations embrace this new frontier, they must view GenAI as more than just a tool for optimization—it is a strategic enabler that redefines how businesses innovate, operate, and compete. By prioritizing adaptability, sustainability, and collaboration, manufacturers can unlock the full potential of GenAI, driving growth and resilience in an increasingly complex and interconnected world.

Key Takeaways

1. **Transformational Efficiency**: GenAI is revolutionizing manufacturing by automating workflows, optimizing production schedules, and reducing waste. From predictive maintenance to automated quality assurance, GenAI-driven systems are enhancing efficiency and minimizing downtime, enabling manufacturers to maximize productivity while lowering operational costs.

2. **Sustainability Gains**: GenAI plays a critical role in helping manufacturers meet environmental goals. By analyzing energy consumption, material usage, and production processes, GenAI provides actionable insights to minimize waste and reduce carbon footprints. These capabilities align manufacturing operations with sustainability objectives, improving compliance and enhancing brand reputation.

3. **Enhanced Decision-Making**: GenAI enables manufacturers to make real-time, data-driven decisions by processing vast amounts of information and providing actionable insights. This capability improves demand forecasting, resource allocation, and supply chain management, ensuring manufacturers can adapt to market changes and disruptions with agility.

4. **Reskilled Workforce**: The integration of GenAI is transforming workforce roles, emphasizing the need for upskilling in AI tools, data analytics, and human-AI collaboration. New roles such as AI Operations Engineers and Predictive Maintenance Analysts are emerging, highlighting the growing importance of technical expertise and adaptability in modern manufacturing.

5. **Resilience and Agility**: By providing real-time insights into supply chain dynamics and production workflows, GenAI enhances operational resilience and agility. Manufacturers can anticipate and respond to disruptions more effectively, ensuring continuity and competitiveness in a rapidly changing global market.

Rick Abbott

As GenAI continues to transform the manufacturing landscape, organizations must embrace this technology as a strategic enabler of growth, efficiency, and sustainability. The potential for operational excellence is immense, but realizing it requires deliberate investment in training, robust governance frameworks, and the integration of AI-driven tools into existing systems. Manufacturers that act swiftly and strategically will not only secure a competitive edge but also play a pivotal role in shaping the future of the industry. By aligning technological innovation with ethical practices and workforce empowerment, the manufacturing sector can unlock the full promise of GenAI and drive meaningful progress for businesses and society alike.

CHAPTER 5: HEALTHCARE

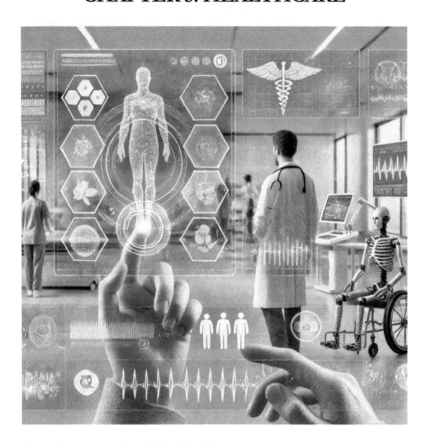

Introduction to GenAI in Healthcare

Healthcare is a cornerstone of societal well-being, ensuring the prevention, diagnosis, and treatment of illnesses while promoting overall health and longevity. From primary care and emergency response to specialized treatments and chronic disease management, the healthcare sector serves as a critical pillar of public infrastructure. As global health challenges evolve—ranging from aging populations to emerging diseases—the demand for innovative approaches to enhance efficiency, accuracy, and accessibility has never been greater.

High-Level Explanation of GenAI's Relevance to Healthcare

GenAI has emerged as a transformative technology in healthcare, revolutionizing the way medical professionals deliver care and patients experience treatment. Unlike traditional AI, which primarily focuses on classification and prediction, GenAI excels at generating new, meaningful insights from complex datasets, making it an invaluable tool for healthcare providers and researchers. By analyzing patterns in medical records, imaging data, and genomic information, GenAI can assist in early disease detection, propose tailored treatment plans, and support decision-making with data-driven recommendations.

GenAI enhances operational efficiency by automating time-consuming administrative tasks such as documentation, coding, and patient scheduling. It supports personalized medicine by integrating diverse data sources—from wearable health devices to genetic profiles—to create customized care pathways. GenAI's applications extend to telehealth, where AI-powered virtual assistants facilitate remote consultations and enhance patient accessibility. This multifaceted impact underscores the potential of GenAI to bridge gaps in healthcare delivery, improve outcomes, and address disparities across populations.

Current Challenges or Gaps That GenAI Can Address

The healthcare industry faces significant challenges that impede the delivery of optimal care. One of the most pressing issues is diagnostic inaccuracy, which can lead to delayed treatment and adverse patient outcomes. Traditional diagnostic methods often rely heavily on human expertise, which, while invaluable, is subject to limitations such as cognitive biases and workload pressures. GenAI addresses these challenges by leveraging advanced pattern recognition capabilities to analyze medical imaging, lab results, and symptom data with unprecedented precision, enabling earlier and more accurate diagnoses.

Another critical gap lies in the personalization of treatment. Despite advancements in medical science, many treatment protocols follow a one-size-fits-all approach, neglecting individual variability in genetics, lifestyle, and environmental factors. GenAI's ability to synthesize and interpret complex datasets allows for the development of personalized treatment strategies that align with each patient's unique profile, improving efficacy and reducing side effects.

Healthcare accessibility remains a global concern, particularly in underserved and rural areas where resources are limited. GenAI-powered telehealth platforms and virtual assistants enable patients to receive timely medical advice, schedule appointments, and even monitor chronic conditions without the need for in-person visits. By addressing these challenges, GenAI not only augments the capabilities of healthcare providers but also democratizes access to quality care, ensuring that advancements in medical technology benefit all segments of the population.

Transformational Impact

GenAI is revolutionizing healthcare by introducing innovative solutions that enhance diagnostic accuracy, streamline treatment plans, and improve patient outcomes. In diagnostics, GenAI's ability to process and analyze medical imaging—such as X-rays, MRIs, and CT scans—enables earlier and more accurate detection of conditions ranging from fractures to cancer. These advancements not only reduce diagnostic errors but also allow for timely interventions that can save lives. GenAI supports predictive analytics, helping healthcare providers forecast disease progression and tailor interventions accordingly.

In treatment, GenAI facilitates the creation of personalized medicine by integrating genomic data, patient history, and real-time health metrics. This enables the design of customized therapeutic regimens that consider individual variability, leading to better efficacy and reduced side effects. For example, AI-driven platforms can recommend medication adjustments based on genetic predispositions or detect potential adverse drug interactions before they occur. This level of personalization transforms patient care, making it more precise and effective.

Patient monitoring is another area where GenAI is having a profound impact. Wearable devices and IoT-enabled sensors generate continuous streams of health data, which GenAI systems analyze to identify anomalies and predict potential health crises. Alerts for conditions like arrhythmias or sudden drops in blood sugar levels can be sent to both patients and healthcare providers, enabling rapid responses that prevent complications.

Changes in Workflows, Decision-Making, and Team Dynamics

The adoption of GenAI in healthcare is reshaping workflows, decision-making processes, and team dynamics. Traditional workflows that relied heavily on manual data entry, analysis, and reporting are now augmented or replaced by AI-driven automation. For instance, administrative tasks such as appointment scheduling, medical transcription, and billing are streamlined through GenAI tools, freeing up healthcare professionals to focus on patient care. Decision-making has become more data-driven, with AI providing actionable insights that support clinical judgments and reduce cognitive burden.

Team dynamics are evolving as interdisciplinary collaboration becomes essential to leverage GenAI effectively. Physicians, data scientists, and IT professionals work together to implement and refine AI systems, ensuring they meet clinical needs and ethical standards. This collaboration fosters a more integrated approach to patient care, where technology complements human expertise rather than replacing it.

Shift in Focus or Priorities Due to GenAI Adoption

The integration of GenAI has shifted healthcare's focus toward proactive and preventive care. By identifying risks before they escalate into critical conditions, GenAI empowers providers to intervene early, reducing the burden on emergency services and improving long-term patient outcomes. Additionally, healthcare systems are increasingly prioritizing patient-centric care, using GenAI to tailor treatments and enhance the overall patient experience. This shift also underscores the importance of continuous education and upskilling for medical professionals to adapt to an AI-enhanced environment.

Top Opportunities for GenAI in Healthcare

- **Enhanced Diagnostic Precision**: GenAI's advanced pattern recognition capabilities improve the accuracy and speed of diagnosing conditions such as cancer, cardiovascular diseases, and rare disorders.
- **Personalized Treatment Plans**: Integrating genomic and lifestyle data, GenAI designs individualized therapeutic strategies that maximize efficacy and minimize adverse effects.
- **Real-Time Patient Monitoring**: AI-powered analysis of wearable device data enables early detection of health issues and timely interventions.
- **Drug Discovery Acceleration**: GenAI reduces the time and cost of developing new drugs by identifying promising compounds and simulating their effects.
- **Healthcare Accessibility**: Virtual health assistants powered by GenAI provide remote consultations and health monitoring, bridging gaps in underserved regions.

GenAI is reshaping healthcare by enhancing precision, personalization, and accessibility. Its ability to analyze complex datasets, predict outcomes, and automate workflows positions it as a transformative force in diagnostics, treatment, and patient care. By fostering collaboration between technology and healthcare professionals, GenAI paves the way for a future where medical advancements benefit all.

Key Technologies and Tools

GenAI leverages advanced models and platforms that have become integral to modern healthcare. Tools such as natural language processing (NLP) systems analyze unstructured data from electronic health records (EHRs), while computer vision algorithms interpret medical imaging to detect abnormalities with high accuracy. Predictive analytics platforms integrate patient histories, genomic data, and real-time health metrics to generate actionable insights for treatment and care. These technologies collectively enable more efficient and effective healthcare delivery.

Integration With Existing Technologies

The seamless integration of GenAI into existing healthcare systems is critical for maximizing its potential. GenAI-enhanced EHRs allow clinicians to access summarized patient histories, identify trends, and prioritize care based on AI-driven risk assessments. Integrating GenAI with telehealth platforms enhances virtual consultations by providing real-time diagnostic support and tailored recommendations. Wearable devices and IoT-enabled sensors feed continuous data streams into GenAI systems, enabling proactive monitoring and early intervention.

Collaboration across healthcare ecosystems is also essential for successful integration. GenAI platforms must interface with laboratory information systems (LIS), radiology systems (RIS), and pharmacy management software to ensure interoperability. Advanced APIs facilitate data exchange, enabling a holistic view of patient health and supporting coordinated care across providers. By aligning GenAI tools with existing workflows, healthcare organizations can achieve greater efficiency and improve patient outcomes.

Technical Trends Influencing Healthcare

Several key technical trends are shaping the adoption and impact of GenAI in healthcare:

- **AI-Powered Imaging Tools**: Advanced image recognition models improve diagnostic accuracy in radiology and pathology, enabling earlier detection of diseases such as cancer.
- **Genomic Data Integration**: The integration of genetic data with clinical records allows for the development of precision medicine tailored to individual patient profiles.
- **Wearable Tech and IoT**: Devices that monitor vital signs and activity levels provide continuous data streams that GenAI systems analyze for real-time health insights.
- **Telehealth Optimization**: GenAI enhances telehealth by supporting remote diagnostics, automating follow-up scheduling, and improving access to care.
- **Healthcare Data Interoperability**: Efforts to standardize data formats and improve interoperability enable seamless sharing of patient information across platforms, enhancing care coordination.

By leveraging these technologies and trends, GenAI continues to drive innovation in healthcare, ensuring more precise, personalized, and accessible care for patients worldwide.

Challenges and Risks

The adoption of GenAI in healthcare brings unique ethical challenges, particularly regarding data privacy and security. Patient records often contain sensitive information, and the integration of GenAI into healthcare systems increases the volume of data shared across platforms. This raises concerns about unauthorized access, data breaches, and compliance with regulations like HIPAA. Ensuring robust security measures is paramount to protecting patient confidentiality and trust.

Bias in AI diagnostic models is another pressing ethical concern. These models are trained on historical datasets, which may reflect existing biases in healthcare systems, such as underrepresentation of certain demographic groups. If unchecked, this bias can lead to disparities in diagnosis and treatment, disproportionately affecting marginalized populations. Addressing these biases requires continuous auditing and refinement of AI systems to promote fairness and equity in healthcare delivery.

Risks of Misuse or Dependency on GenAI

Over-reliance on GenAI systems presents significant risks, including the potential for inaccuracies or misdiagnoses. While GenAI enhances diagnostic precision, it is not infallible and can produce errors if the underlying data is flawed or incomplete. Healthcare professionals must maintain a balance between leveraging AI insights and exercising their clinical judgment to ensure patient safety.

Another risk is the misuse of GenAI technologies. For example, malicious actors could exploit AI systems to fabricate medical records or manipulate healthcare data, leading to misinformation and compromised patient care. Strengthening oversight mechanisms and implementing stringent controls can mitigate these risks and ensure that GenAI is used responsibly.

Frameworks or Guidelines to Address Risks

To address these challenges and risks, healthcare organizations should adopt comprehensive frameworks and guidelines, including:

- **Bias Detection Protocols**: Implement tools to identify and correct biases in AI models, ensuring equitable treatment across diverse patient populations.
- **Data Privacy Safeguards**: Strengthen encryption and access controls to protect sensitive patient data and comply with regulatory standards.
- **Transparent AI Systems**: Develop algorithms that provide interpretable results, allowing healthcare professionals to understand and validate AI-driven recommendations.
- **Regulatory Compliance Models**: Align AI implementations with existing healthcare regulations, such as HIPAA and GDPR, to maintain legal and ethical standards.
- **Human Oversight Integration**: Ensure that healthcare professionals remain integral to decision-making processes, using GenAI as a tool to complement, not replace, their expertise.

Addressing the challenges and risks associated with the integration of GenAI in healthcare requires a proactive, multifaceted approach. By prioritizing ethical considerations, such as mitigating biases in AI models and safeguarding sensitive patient data, healthcare organizations can ensure that these technologies are implemented responsibly. Establishing robust frameworks for human oversight and transparent decision-making not only minimizes risks of dependency or misuse but also reinforces trust among patients and stakeholders. Through collaboration across regulatory, clinical, and technical domains, the healthcare sector can harness the transformative potential of GenAI while navigating its complexities with integrity and foresight. Ultimately, the responsible adoption of GenAI will enable healthcare systems to deliver safer, more personalized, and equitable care, ensuring that advancements benefit all segments of society.

Skillset Evolution

The integration of GenAI into healthcare is reshaping the skill requirements for professionals across the industry. Healthcare providers now need to develop AI literacy to understand and interact with GenAI tools effectively. This involves learning how to interpret AI-driven insights, validate recommendations, and integrate them into clinical decision-making. Technical skills such as data analysis and familiarity with AI platforms are becoming increasingly important, alongside traditional clinical expertise.

Training and Upskilling Needs

To adapt to these changes, healthcare professionals require comprehensive training programs focused on GenAI applications. This includes workshops on data handling, AI ethics, and the principles of machine learning to build foundational knowledge. Clinicians may also need to engage in role-specific training, such as using AI in diagnostic imaging or personalized treatment planning. Collaboration with data scientists and IT specialists during training fosters a multidisciplinary approach that bridges the gap between clinical care and technology.

Upskilling programs must also address the ethical and regulatory aspects of AI use. Ensuring that professionals are equipped to handle issues like patient privacy, algorithmic bias, and informed consent is critical to maintaining trust and integrity in AI-enhanced healthcare. Continuous education initiatives will be vital as GenAI technology evolves, ensuring that healthcare providers stay current with the latest advancements and best practices.

Potential for New Roles or Career Paths

The adoption of GenAI is creating new career opportunities in the healthcare sector. Emerging roles include:

- **AI-Assisted Diagnostic Specialist**: Experts in leveraging AI for interpreting diagnostic tests, ensuring accuracy, and improving patient outcomes.
- **Healthcare Data Scientist**: Professionals who analyze and manage healthcare data to train and refine GenAI models.
- **Telehealth Coordinator with AI Expertise**: Specialists who optimize remote healthcare delivery using AI-driven tools for diagnostics and patient engagement.
- **Ethical AI Advisor in Healthcare**: Advisors who ensure that AI applications adhere to ethical guidelines and regulations, promoting fairness and transparency.
- **Personalized Medicine Specialist**: Clinicians focusing on designing and implementing treatment strategies tailored to individual patients using AI insights.

The evolving role of GenAI in healthcare is redefining the skills and expertise required for professionals across the industry. As AI literacy becomes a fundamental necessity, healthcare workers must balance their clinical knowledge with new technical and ethical competencies to fully leverage the potential of GenAI. Comprehensive training programs and upskilling initiatives will be essential to bridge gaps in knowledge, fostering a multidisciplinary approach that integrates data science and clinical care. The emergence of specialized roles underscores the profound career opportunities GenAI presents, signaling a transformative shift in how healthcare professionals contribute to patient care. By embracing this evolution, the healthcare workforce can not only adapt to the demands of AI-enhanced environments but also drive innovation, ensuring the delivery of safer, more effective, and equitable care.

Emerging Trends

The long-term impact of GenAI on healthcare is poised to be transformative, driving a paradigm shift in how care is delivered and managed. GenAI is expected to integrate deeper into the healthcare ecosystem, enabling predictive, preventive, and precision medicine. By harnessing real-time data from diverse sources such as IoT devices, genomic databases, and EHRs, GenAI will enhance early detection of diseases, optimize resource allocation, and improve patient outcomes. The future of healthcare will likely center around

AI-enabled personalized care that reduces costs and expands accessibility.

Emerging Trends and Their Potential Influence

Several emerging trends highlight how GenAI is shaping the future of healthcare:

- **Predictive Health Analytics**: AI models will continue to improve in forecasting disease onset and progression, empowering clinicians to focus on prevention and early intervention.
- **AI-Driven Clinical Trials**: GenAI will streamline drug development by identifying optimal patient populations, simulating trials, and accelerating the discovery of new treatments.
- **Digital Twins in Medicine**: Virtual replicas of patients will allow healthcare providers to simulate treatments and predict outcomes, tailoring care to individual needs.
- **Augmented Decision Support**: Advanced AI systems will provide clinicians with enhanced diagnostic and treatment recommendations, significantly improving decision-making processes.
- **AI-Enhanced Patient Engagement**: Chatbots, virtual assistants, and other AI-powered tools will foster better communication and engagement between patients and healthcare providers, improving adherence to care plans.

Strategic Priorities for Organizations to Stay Competitive

To remain at the forefront of innovation, healthcare organizations must focus on key strategic priorities:

- **Investing in AI Infrastructure**: Develop robust technological foundations, including scalable AI platforms and secure data repositories, to support GenAI implementations.
- **Promoting Interoperability**: Foster seamless data exchange between systems and organizations to unlock the full potential of GenAI applications.
- **Focusing on Patient-Centric Care**: Use GenAI to prioritize personalized care approaches and ensure patient outcomes remain the central focus.

- **Building Ethical AI Frameworks**: Implement governance structures to address concerns around bias, privacy, and accountability in GenAI systems.
- **Enhancing Workforce Skills**: Equip healthcare professionals with the training and tools needed to effectively integrate AI into their workflows.

The transformative potential of GenAI in healthcare is becoming increasingly clear as emerging trends and strategic priorities shape its integration into the industry. By leveraging predictive analytics, digital twins, and AI-driven patient engagement, GenAI is poised to revolutionize care delivery and patient outcomes. Realizing these advancements will require healthcare organizations to invest in robust AI infrastructure, promote interoperability, and prioritize ethical practices. As the focus shifts towards patient-centric and precision medicine, the adoption of GenAI will redefine healthcare as a more proactive, personalized, and accessible system. Embracing these changes with strategic foresight will ensure that the benefits of GenAI are maximized while addressing the complexities of its implementation.

Conclusion

GenAI is transforming the healthcare industry by addressing critical challenges and driving innovation across diagnostics, treatment personalization, and patient care. Its ability to analyze complex datasets, automate workflows, and provide actionable insights has established it as an indispensable tool for healthcare providers. By bridging gaps in care delivery, enhancing operational efficiency, and enabling more personalized and proactive approaches, GenAI is reshaping the future of healthcare.

Emphasis on the Need for Strategic Thinking and Adaptability

To fully harness the transformative power of GenAI, healthcare organizations must adopt a strategic approach. This involves integrating AI systems thoughtfully, addressing ethical and regulatory challenges, and ensuring that the technology complements, rather than replaces, human expertise. Professionals across the industry must remain adaptable, embracing continuous learning to keep pace with technological advancements. By prioritizing patient-centered care, fostering interdisciplinary collaboration, and maintaining a focus on ethical practices, the healthcare sector can maximize the potential of GenAI while safeguarding its integrity.

Key Takeaways

1. **Transforming Diagnostics with Precision**: GenAI significantly enhances diagnostic accuracy by analyzing complex datasets like medical imaging and patient histories. This leads to earlier detection and improved outcomes for conditions ranging from cancer to cardiovascular diseases.
2. **Personalized Medicine**: Leveraging data such as genomics and lifestyle information, GenAI empowers healthcare professionals to design individualized treatment plans, maximizing efficacy while minimizing risks.
3. **Operational Efficiency**: By automating administrative tasks and optimizing workflows, GenAI allows healthcare providers to focus more on patient care, improving overall system efficiency.
4. **Ethical and Regulatory Considerations**: Effective integration of GenAI into healthcare requires addressing challenges like data privacy, algorithmic bias, and transparency, supported by frameworks that ensure fairness and compliance.
5. **Emerging Roles and Trends**: The adoption of GenAI fosters new career paths, including roles such as AI-assisted diagnostic specialists and ethical AI advisors, while driving long-term trends like predictive health analytics and AI-enhanced patient engagement.

The potential of GenAI in healthcare is vast, offering transformative solutions to age-old challenges while paving the way for innovative care models. However, realizing this potential requires a commitment to ethical practices, continuous learning, and strategic investments in AI infrastructure. Organizations and professionals must work collaboratively to ensure that technological advancements prioritize patient welfare and equity, fostering a future where healthcare is more accessible, precise, and impactful.

CHAPTER 6: EDUCATION

Introduction to GenAI in Education

Education is the foundation of societal progress, equipping individuals with the knowledge, skills, and critical thinking necessary to navigate and contribute to an ever-changing world. From fostering innovation to addressing global challenges, education plays a pivotal role in shaping the future. However, the traditional one-size-fits-all approach often struggles to meet the diverse needs of learners, particularly in an increasingly complex and technology-driven era.

GenAI's Relevance to Education

GenAI is transforming the education landscape by introducing hyper-personalized learning experiences that adapt to the unique requirements of each student. Unlike traditional methods that rely on standardized curricula, GenAI tailors educational content to align with individual learning styles, paces, and preferences. For example, large language models like GPT-4 can generate customized lesson plans, create interactive exercises, and even provide real-time feedback to learners. By leveraging natural language processing (NLP), educators can build engaging, adaptive environments where students receive tailored support and resources.

GenAI is empowering educators by automating repetitive tasks, such as grading and administrative work, freeing them to focus on higher-order teaching strategies. Its ability to analyze vast datasets enables predictive insights, such as identifying at-risk students or optimizing curriculum design based on learning trends. With GenAI, education becomes a dynamic, interactive, and inclusive ecosystem that bridges gaps in accessibility and scalability, making high-quality learning resources available to a global audience.

Current Challenges Addressed by GenAI

Despite the transformative potential of education, the sector faces persistent challenges that hinder its ability to meet the demands of a rapidly evolving world. Scalability is a significant issue, as traditional classrooms are often constrained by teacher-to-student ratios and limited resources. Personalized attention, critical for effective learning, becomes challenging in overcrowded educational settings. GenAI addresses this by automating content delivery and providing individualized learning pathways, enabling educators to cater to diverse student needs without increasing workload.

Another pressing challenge is the inequitable distribution of resources across regions and socioeconomic groups. In underserved areas, students often lack access to quality teaching materials, experienced educators, and modern tools. GenAI bridges this divide by generating cost-effective, high-quality educational content that can be accessed on digital platforms. The rigid structure of traditional education systems often fails to accommodate different learning paces and styles, leaving many students disengaged. GenAI's adaptive technologies foster engagement by delivering content in a variety of formats—text, audio, video, and interactive simulations—ensuring that every learner can access and benefit from education in a way that resonates with them.

By addressing these challenges, GenAI is not only transforming education but also laying the groundwork for a future where learning is equitable, engaging, and personalized for all.

Transformational Impact

GenAI is revolutionizing education by transforming how students learn, teachers teach, and institutions operate. Traditionally, education has relied on fixed curricula and static resources that often fail to address the dynamic needs of learners. GenAI introduces a new paradigm by enabling real-time adaptability in the learning process. For instance, AI-powered platforms can analyze a student's performance, identify areas of difficulty, and generate personalized exercises to address those gaps. This level of customization not only enhances comprehension but also fosters self-directed learning by encouraging students to take ownership of their educational journey.

In addition to enhancing the learner experience, GenAI empowers educators with advanced tools to streamline their workflows and amplify their impact. Tasks such as grading assignments, creating lesson plans, and monitoring student progress are automated, allowing teachers to focus on mentoring and fostering critical thinking. Institutions benefit from data-driven decision-making as GenAI analyzes large datasets to predict enrollment trends, optimize resource allocation, and evaluate program effectiveness. By integrating these capabilities, GenAI creates an education ecosystem that is adaptive, inclusive, and future-ready.

Changes in Workflows and Dynamics

The adoption of GenAI is reshaping the workflows and dynamics within the education sector. Educators are transitioning from content delivery roles to facilitators of learning, leveraging AI tools to provide tailored support and enrich classroom interactions. Workflows that were once time-intensive, such as grading or curriculum planning, can now be automated, freeing educators to concentrate on personalized instruction and student engagement. Students, on the other hand, experience a shift toward active participation as AI tools enable interactive and immersive learning environments.

The integration of GenAI also fosters collaboration between educators and technology, redefining traditional roles and responsibilities. Schools and universities are adopting blended learning models where AI-driven platforms complement human instruction, ensuring that each student receives the best of both worlds. This collaborative approach encourages educators to focus on nurturing creativity, critical thinking, and emotional intelligence—skills that are uniquely human and cannot be replicated by AI.

Rick Abbott
Shift in Focus Due to GenAI Adoption

As GenAI becomes more embedded in education, the sector's priorities are shifting toward engagement, adaptability, and inclusivity. Institutions are prioritizing technologies that enhance student engagement by making learning more interactive and relevant. Real-time adaptability is another focal point, as AI tools continuously adjust to meet the evolving needs of learners. Inclusivity has taken center stage, with GenAI enabling access to high-quality educational resources for students from underserved communities and those with disabilities. By removing barriers to learning, GenAI ensures that education becomes a universally empowering force.

Top Opportunities for GenAI in Education

GenAI presents several key opportunities to revolutionize the education sector:

- **Dynamic Curriculum Generation:** AI-powered platforms create personalized lesson plans tailored to individual learning profiles. This adaptability enhances engagement and ensures students master concepts at their own pace.
- **Real-Time Feedback Systems:** Automated grading and AI-driven insights provide immediate feedback to students, helping them improve and stay motivated. This fosters a culture of continuous learning and growth.
- **Accessible Learning Resources:** GenAI generates content in multiple formats, such as text, audio, and video, making education accessible to learners with varying needs, including those with visual or auditory impairments.
- **Interactive Learning Environments:** Virtual tutors and AI-driven simulations enable hands-on, immersive learning experiences. These tools allow students to experiment, fail safely, and learn through exploration.
- **Predictive Learning Analytics:** By analyzing performance data, GenAI identifies learning patterns and predicts potential challenges. Educators can intervene proactively, enhancing student outcomes and reducing dropout rates.

By fostering personalized learning, automating repetitive tasks, and enhancing accessibility, GenAI is driving a transformative shift in education. It empowers teachers, engages students, and equips institutions with tools to address challenges in real time. As GenAI continues to evolve, its integration into education will redefine traditional models, creating a dynamic, inclusive, and equitable learning ecosystem for all.

Key Technologies and Tools

GenAI is transforming education by introducing a range of advanced tools and models that enhance learning and streamline administrative processes. Key among these are large language models like OpenAI's GPT series, which can generate personalized lesson plans, answer complex questions, and support students with real-time tutoring. Adaptive learning platforms, such as those powered by AI, create customized pathways for students by adjusting the difficulty and type of content based on their progress. Immersive technologies like augmented reality (AR) and virtual reality (VR) provide interactive environments where students can explore subjects hands-on, from virtual science labs to historical reconstructions. These tools collectively make learning more dynamic, engaging, and effective.

Integration with Existing Systems

The successful adoption of GenAI in education depends on its seamless integration with existing technologies, such as Learning Management Systems (LMS) and educational applications. Platforms like Moodle, Blackboard, and Google Classroom can be enhanced with GenAI capabilities to offer tailored content, automate grading, and provide data-driven insights into student performance. For example, integrating GenAI with an LMS allows educators to generate real-time progress reports, identify students who are struggling, and recommend personalized interventions.

GenAI's natural language processing capabilities enable multilingual support, ensuring that students from diverse linguistic backgrounds can access high-quality resources. Integration with mobile applications ensures that learners have access to educational content anytime, anywhere, fostering flexibility and inclusivity. Such seamless interoperability between GenAI and existing systems amplifies its benefits while minimizing disruptions to established workflows.

Technical Trends in Education

Emerging technological trends are reshaping education, with GenAI playing a pivotal role in driving innovation. These trends are enabling more personalized, efficient, and engaging learning experiences:

1. **Adaptive Learning Systems:** AI dynamically adjusts content and pacing based on individual student performance, ensuring personalized learning that keeps pace with each learner's needs.
2. **Multimodal Content Generation:** GenAI creates diverse content types—text, audio, video, and interactive visuals—to cater to varying learning styles and preferences, enhancing comprehension and retention.
3. **Voice-Powered Learning Assistants:** Conversational AI tools act as virtual tutors, answering student queries, providing explanations, and facilitating real-time engagement through natural language interaction.
4. **Gamification of Learning:** AI-driven games adapt in complexity and challenge based on the learner's progress, making education enjoyable and motivating while reinforcing core concepts.
5. **AI-Powered Assessment Tools:** These tools automate grading and generate detailed feedback, enabling educators to focus on providing personalized guidance rather than being bogged down by administrative tasks.

By leveraging these technologies and trends, educational institutions can enhance their ability to deliver personalized, efficient, and innovative learning experiences. As GenAI continues to evolve, its integration with existing systems and emerging tools will redefine the possibilities of modern education.

Challenges and Risks

The integration of GenAI in education brings significant ethical challenges, particularly concerning bias and data privacy. GenAI systems are often trained on large datasets that may inadvertently reflect societal biases, potentially leading to unequal or unfair outcomes in learning recommendations or assessments. For instance, AI-generated content might unintentionally prioritize dominant cultural perspectives, marginalizing underrepresented groups and perpetuating inequities. Ensuring that AI systems are inclusive and unbiased is critical to fostering equitable learning environments.

Data privacy is another pressing concern, as GenAI relies on processing vast amounts of personal information, including student performance metrics, learning preferences, and even behavioral patterns. The potential misuse or unauthorized access to such sensitive data poses serious risks, especially in regions with stringent privacy regulations like GDPR or FERPA. Educational institutions must implement robust security measures and transparent policies to safeguard student data and maintain trust in AI-driven systems.

Risks of Dependency on GenAI

While GenAI offers transformative potential, over-reliance on these systems could introduce risks that undermine the quality of education. One such risk is the reduction of critical thinking and creativity among students. If learners become overly dependent on AI for answers or content creation, they may miss opportunities to develop problem-solving skills and independent thought processes. Teachers relying heavily on AI for grading or curriculum design might lose touch with the nuances of student needs that require human empathy and judgment.

Another concern is the potential erosion of teacher-student relationships. The dynamic interaction between educators and students fosters mentorship, emotional support, and personalized guidance—elements that cannot be fully replicated by AI. A balance must be maintained to ensure that GenAI enhances rather than replaces these vital human connections.

Technical risks also exist, including system errors, biased outputs, and lack of transparency in GenAI decision-making processes. If educators cannot understand or validate how AI tools reach certain conclusions, their ability to trust and effectively use these tools may diminish. Technological failures, such as software bugs or outages, could disrupt learning experiences and erode confidence in AI systems.

Mitigation Frameworks

To address these challenges and risks, educational institutions can adopt comprehensive mitigation frameworks that ensure the ethical, secure, and effective implementation of GenAI. The following approaches can help navigate potential pitfalls:

- **Bias Audits:** Regularly review and test AI systems for biases in recommendations, assessments, and content generation. Diverse datasets and inclusive training protocols can help mitigate systemic inequities.

- **Transparent AI Practices:** Communicate clearly about how GenAI is used in educational processes. Students, parents, and educators should understand the role of AI and have access to explanations of its decision-making processes.
- **Data Security Measures:** Implement robust encryption, anonymization, and access controls to protect student information. Compliance with data protection regulations like GDPR and FERPA is essential for maintaining trust and legal compliance.
- **Human Oversight:** Retain educators as key decision-makers, ensuring that AI tools support rather than replace their roles. Human oversight ensures accountability, empathy, and adaptability in teaching and assessment.
- **AI Literacy Programs:** Train teachers, administrators, and students in understanding and responsibly using AI tools. Familiarity with GenAI fosters informed usage and reduces over-reliance on technology.

By proactively addressing these challenges and implementing mitigation strategies, educational institutions can ensure that GenAI is used responsibly and effectively. This balanced approach preserves the human-centric values of education while unlocking the transformative potential of AI.

Skillset Evolution

As GenAI becomes integral to education, the skills required of educators, administrators, and even students are evolving rapidly. Traditional teaching methods, heavily reliant on content delivery, are giving way to roles that emphasize facilitation, guidance, and the integration of AI-driven tools. Teachers must develop AI literacy, enabling them to use GenAI to design curricula, provide personalized learning experiences, and interpret data-driven insights. Administrators, in turn, need to harness AI analytics for strategic decision-making, resource allocation, and enhancing institutional performance.

For students, the ability to collaborate effectively with AI systems is emerging as a critical competency. This includes understanding how to frame questions, evaluate AI-generated content, and apply insights to problem-solving. These shifts highlight the growing importance of technical proficiency, critical thinking, and adaptability as foundational skills in the AI-driven educational landscape.

Training Needs

To thrive in this evolving environment, educators and administrators require targeted professional development programs. These programs should focus on building foundational knowledge of AI technologies, including how GenAI functions, its limitations, and its potential applications in education. Practical training on tools like adaptive learning platforms, automated assessment systems, and interactive content generation tools is essential for educators to implement AI effectively in their classrooms.

Beyond technical training, programs must emphasize the ethical use of AI. Teachers and administrators need to understand how to identify and mitigate biases in AI systems, ensure data privacy, and maintain transparency in their use of AI tools. By embedding these considerations into professional development, institutions can foster a culture of responsible AI use.

Training initiatives should also encourage collaboration among educators, technologists, and policymakers to share best practices and innovative approaches. Workshops, webinars, and hands-on sessions tailored to different levels of expertise will ensure that all stakeholders are equipped to integrate GenAI effectively. Continuous learning is key, as AI technologies and educational strategies evolve rapidly, requiring ongoing adaptation and skill enhancement.

Emerging Roles

The adoption of GenAI is creating new career opportunities within education, blending traditional expertise with emerging technological capabilities. Below are five key roles that exemplify the evolving landscape of education:

- **AI Curriculum Designer:** Professionals in this role leverage GenAI to create adaptive lesson plans, interactive exercises, and personalized content tailored to diverse learner needs. Their expertise combines pedagogy with AI tools to enhance engagement and comprehension.
- **Learning Analytics Specialist:** These specialists analyze AI-driven insights to identify trends, assess student performance, and recommend data-informed interventions. Their work enables institutions to optimize learning outcomes and allocate resources efficiently.

- **AI Ethics Advisor in Education:** Tasked with ensuring the ethical use of AI tools, these advisors monitor systems for bias, protect student privacy, and develop guidelines for responsible AI implementation. They play a vital role in maintaining trust and transparency.

- **Virtual Learning Facilitator:** These educators manage AI-driven remote learning environments, ensuring seamless delivery of content and addressing student needs in real-time. They focus on building engaging, collaborative, and inclusive virtual classrooms.

- **AI-Enhanced Instructional Designer:** This role involves integrating AI tools into instructional strategies, such as gamified learning, virtual labs, and immersive simulations. By combining AI capabilities with traditional teaching methods, these designers create transformative educational experiences.

The integration of GenAI into education is reshaping the roles and responsibilities of educators and administrators, while opening new career paths. By investing in training and embracing these emerging opportunities, institutions can empower their workforce to lead the transformation of education into a more personalized, engaging, and effective system.

Emerging Trends

The integration of GenAI into education is expected to bring transformative, long-lasting effects. Traditional classrooms will evolve into dynamic, personalized learning environments where technology and instruction work in harmony. AI-driven personalization will empower students to learn at their own pace, bridging gaps in achievement and fostering a culture of lifelong learning. The accessibility of AI-powered tools will expand global access to quality education, enabling underserved communities to benefit from tailored resources and interactive experiences. Over time, GenAI is likely to redefine education's role in society, equipping learners with the skills needed for an AI-driven world while emphasizing critical thinking, creativity, and adaptability.

The rapid development of GenAI has catalyzed several emerging trends that are reshaping the education landscape:

- **Micro-Certifications and AI-Assisted Lifelong Learning:** GenAI is facilitating the rise of micro-certifications and modular learning paths, allowing students to acquire specific skills quickly and effectively. AI-driven platforms can analyze industry trends and individual career goals to recommend targeted learning modules. This trend supports the shift toward lifelong learning, enabling learners to upskill and reskill as needed in a dynamic job market.

- **Augmented Reality (AR) and Virtual Reality (VR) in Learning:** AI-powered AR and VR technologies are creating immersive, hands-on learning experiences that were previously impossible in traditional settings. From virtual science labs to historical reconstructions, these tools enhance engagement and comprehension by placing learners in interactive, real-world scenarios.

- **Cultural Sensitivity in AI Models:** As education becomes increasingly globalized, there is a growing demand for AI models to be culturally sensitive and inclusive. GenAI tools are being developed to localize content, ensuring that it aligns with diverse linguistic, cultural, and social contexts. This trend promotes inclusivity and relevance in educational materials.

- **Proactive Learning Interventions:** Predictive analytics powered by GenAI enables educators to identify students at risk of falling behind and implement timely interventions. By analyzing learning patterns, engagement levels, and assessment data, AI tools can recommend personalized support strategies, improving retention and outcomes.

- **Ethical AI Adoption in Education:** As reliance on GenAI grows, there is an increasing focus on developing ethical frameworks to ensure responsible implementation. This includes addressing issues like data privacy, algorithmic transparency, and bias mitigation. Institutions are adopting policies and best practices to foster trust and accountability in AI-driven education systems.

Strategic Priorities

To maximize the benefits of GenAI while addressing challenges, educational institutions must adopt forward-thinking strategies. The following priorities can guide the successful integration of AI into education:

- **Scalable AI Platforms:** Invest in scalable and interoperable AI platforms that can adapt to the evolving needs of institutions and learners. Scalable systems ensure that AI tools remain effective as student populations and technological demands grow.

- **Inclusive Content Creation:** Develop AI-generated content that is accessible to all learners, including those with disabilities and those from diverse cultural backgrounds. Inclusive content ensures equity in education and fosters a more connected learning community.
- **Data-Driven Decision-Making:** Leverage AI analytics to inform policy, curriculum design, and resource allocation. By making data-driven decisions, institutions can optimize their operations and improve student outcomes.
- **Partnerships with EdTech Providers:** Collaborate with EdTech companies to co-develop innovative solutions that align with institutional goals. Partnerships can accelerate the adoption of cutting-edge technologies while addressing specific educational challenges.
- **Continuous Research and Development:** Commit to ongoing research into the applications and implications of GenAI in education. By staying at the forefront of technological advancements, institutions can anticipate future trends and remain competitive.

By embracing these trends and strategic priorities, educational institutions can harness the transformative potential of GenAI to create more adaptive, inclusive, and effective learning environments.

Conclusion

GenAI is revolutionizing education by addressing long-standing challenges and creating new opportunities for personalized, accessible, and engaging learning experiences. From automating repetitive tasks to providing real-time feedback and generating adaptive curricula, GenAI empowers educators and students alike. It enhances the efficiency of educational processes, bridges resource gaps, and fosters a dynamic, inclusive environment where every learner can thrive. As educational institutions integrate GenAI, they are transforming traditional classrooms into innovative ecosystems capable of preparing students for a rapidly changing world.

Need for Strategic Adoption

The potential of GenAI in education is immense, but its successful implementation requires strategic planning and thoughtful execution.

Institutions must adopt GenAI as a complementary tool rather than a replacement for human educators, ensuring that it amplifies human creativity and empathy rather than diminishing it. Transparency in AI decision-making, robust data security protocols, and a commitment to ethical use are critical to maintaining trust and fairness in educational practices. By fostering a culture of collaboration between technology and pedagogy, institutions can create a balanced approach that combines AI's capabilities with the irreplaceable value of human connection in education.

Continuous professional development is essential to equip educators and administrators with the skills needed to harness GenAI effectively. Training programs should emphasize not only technical proficiency but also the importance of ethical considerations and cultural sensitivity. As the role of educators evolves, their ability to navigate AI tools responsibly and creatively will determine the long-term success of GenAI in education.

As educational institutions embrace this transformative technology, they must also remain agile and adaptable to the evolving landscape of AI. By investing in research, fostering partnerships with EdTech providers, and maintaining a learner-centric approach, they can ensure that GenAI continues to serve as a force for progress. The journey toward AI-driven education is not just about adopting new tools; it is about reimagining the possibilities of learning itself.

Key Takeaways

1. **Transformative Power of GenAI in Education**: GenAI is revolutionizing education by enabling personalized learning, real-time adaptability, and global accessibility. Its ability to tailor content, automate administrative tasks, and provide predictive insights empowers educators to focus on mentorship and creativity while ensuring students receive individualized support.
2. **Addressing Educational Challenges**: GenAI addresses critical challenges such as inequitable resource distribution, limited scalability, and disengagement by creating cost-effective, dynamic, and inclusive learning environments. It bridges gaps in traditional systems by providing diverse learners with tools to succeed at their own pace and style.
3. **Ethical and Technical Considerations**: The integration of GenAI in education comes with ethical challenges, including bias, data privacy, and transparency. Institutions must adopt

robust frameworks to mitigate these risks, ensuring fair, secure, and trustworthy AI implementation while maintaining a human-centered approach to teaching and learning.

4. **Evolving Skillsets and Roles**: The adoption of GenAI is reshaping the skills required for educators, administrators, and students. Teachers must embrace AI literacy, while new roles such as AI Curriculum Designers and Learning Analytics Specialists are emerging. Continuous upskilling and ethical AI training are critical to navigating this transformation successfully.

5. **Strategic Priorities for the Future of Education:** To harness the full potential of GenAI, educational institutions should focus on scalable AI platforms, inclusive content creation, data-driven decision-making, and partnerships with EdTech providers. By fostering a culture of continuous research and innovation, they can remain agile and adapt to future trends.

GenAI offers a transformative opportunity to reimagine education, making it more inclusive, engaging, and future-ready. To achieve this vision, institutions, educators, and policymakers must collaborate to ensure thoughtful implementation that balances AI's capabilities with human values. By embracing this new frontier, education can evolve into a dynamic force that empowers learners and prepares them for the challenges of tomorrow.

CHAPTER 7: FINANCE AND BANKING

Introduction to GenAI in Finance and Banking

The finance and banking industry serves as the backbone of the global economy, facilitating capital flows, managing risks, and fostering economic growth. From enabling individuals to secure loans for homes and businesses to overseeing complex international transactions, financial institutions are integral to maintaining economic stability. As the sector navigates rapid digital transformation and increasing customer expectations, its role has grown beyond traditional financial services to encompass innovation, accessibility, and security.

GenAI's Relevance to Finance and Banking

GenAI is revolutionizing the finance and banking industry by introducing unprecedented capabilities for data analysis, customer personalization, and operational efficiency. In a domain where accuracy, speed, and trust are paramount, GenAI delivers cutting-edge solutions to long-standing challenges. For instance, AI-powered chatbots provide 24/7 customer support, offering personalized advice based on a client's financial history and preferences. Beyond customer interaction, GenAI excels in analyzing massive datasets to identify patterns, enabling real-time fraud detection and credit risk assessments that were previously unattainable.

The versatility of GenAI extends to automating routine processes, such as compliance reporting and transaction monitoring, reducing costs while improving accuracy. Its ability to create predictive financial models allows institutions to anticipate market trends and adapt strategies accordingly. This transformative technology not only enhances internal operations but also redefines how financial services are delivered, making them more accessible and tailored to individual needs.

Challenges and Gaps Addressed by GenAI

The finance and banking sector faces persistent challenges that hinder efficiency and innovation. Fraud and cybersecurity threats are ever-present, with increasingly sophisticated tactics targeting sensitive financial systems. GenAI addresses these vulnerabilities through advanced anomaly detection, enabling real-time identification and mitigation of suspicious activities.

Regulatory compliance is another major hurdle, with institutions required to navigate complex and evolving frameworks. GenAI simplifies this process by automating data validation and ensuring adherence to regulations through intelligent monitoring systems. Traditional approaches to customer service often fall short in delivering personalized, timely support. By leveraging GenAI, banks can provide individualized financial advice, creating a more engaging and satisfying customer experience.

As the finance and banking industry continues to evolve, Gen AI stands out as a transformative force, addressing critical pain points while unlocking new opportunities for growth and innovation.

Transformational Impact

GenAI is fundamentally altering the landscape of finance and banking, enabling institutions to operate with greater efficiency, precision, and customer-centricity. One of its most significant contributions is in **fraud detection**, where GenAI models analyze transaction patterns and detect anomalies in real time, preventing potential financial crimes. These systems learn continuously from vast datasets, identifying suspicious behaviors that traditional rule-based systems might miss.

In **personalized banking**, GenAI enables a tailored approach to customer engagement. Virtual assistants powered by AI can provide instant financial advice, recommend suitable products, and even guide users through complex decisions like mortgage applications or investment strategies. This level of personalization fosters stronger relationships with customers and enhances satisfaction. Moreover, AI-driven credit risk assessments offer a more nuanced and equitable evaluation of potential borrowers, ensuring that financial products are accessible to underserved populations.

Changes in Workflows, Decision-Making, and Team Dynamics

The integration of GenAI into finance and banking has streamlined workflows by automating time-consuming manual tasks such as data entry, compliance checks, and account reconciliation. These efficiencies free up employees to focus on higher-value activities, such as strategy development and client relationship management. Decision-making processes have also become more data-driven, as AI-powered insights provide financial institutions with actionable intelligence in real time. Teams are now embracing a collaborative dynamic, leveraging AI tools as "co-pilots" that complement human expertise and creativity.

The Shift in Focus or Priorities Due to GenAI Adoption

With GenAI at the forefront, the focus in finance and banking is shifting from reactive problem-solving to proactive risk management and customer engagement. Institutions are prioritizing real-time monitoring and predictive capabilities, enabling them to address potential issues before they escalate. Customer experience has also become a central priority, with GenAI facilitating personalized interactions and services that meet individual needs. This shift underscores the growing recognition of AI as a strategic enabler rather than merely a tool for operational efficiency.

Top Opportunities for Meaningful Impact

- **Fraud Prevention**: GenAI detects anomalies across millions of transactions in real time, flagging suspicious activities and preventing financial losses. Its continuous learning capabilities ensure that fraud detection systems evolve alongside emerging threats.
- **Credit Scoring Revolution**: AI-driven models provide more accurate and unbiased credit assessments, reducing risk for lenders while expanding access to financial products for underserved populations.
- **Personalized Financial Services**: By analyzing customer data, GenAI offers tailored recommendations for investments, loans, and savings plans, enhancing customer loyalty and satisfaction.
- **Regulatory Compliance Automation**: GenAI automates compliance processes, ensuring that institutions adhere to evolving regulatory requirements while reducing the cost and complexity of audits.
- **Operational Optimization**: From automating back-office functions to streamlining supply chains in financial services, GenAI improves efficiency and reduces operational costs.

GenAI is revolutionizing the finance and banking sector by enhancing fraud detection, streamlining compliance, and enabling hyper-personalized customer experiences. As institutions increasingly adopt AI-driven technologies, they are not only optimizing operations but also reimagining their roles in fostering financial inclusivity and innovation. This transformative potential positions GenAI as a critical driver of progress in the financial industry.

Key Technologies and Tools

GenAI has introduced a suite of cutting-edge technologies that are reshaping the finance and banking sector. Key tools include **large language models (LLMs)** like OpenAI's GPT, which can generate human-like text for personalized customer interactions and automated reporting. Predictive analytics platforms such as SAS and Google Cloud AI are also essential, enabling real-time risk assessments and fraud detection. Specialized tools like IBM Watson Finance and Salesforce Einstein cater to industry-specific needs, offering tailored solutions for customer engagement, compliance, and operational optimization.

Integration with Existing Systems

The integration of GenAI with existing banking systems is critical for leveraging its full potential. Many financial institutions rely on legacy systems such as **Customer Relationship Management (CRM)** platforms and **Enterprise Resource Planning (ERP)** tools. By embedding GenAI capabilities, these systems can transform workflows, improve scalability, and enhance decision-making.

For example:

- **CRM Enhancements**: Integrating GenAI with platforms like Salesforce allows for automated customer segmentation, personalized marketing campaigns, and predictive behavior analysis. AI-powered chatbots embedded within these systems offer instant, tailored support.
- **ERP Integration**: AI capabilities embedded in ERP platforms like SAP S/4HANA streamline compliance reporting and automate financial reconciliations. This reduces manual effort and increases accuracy across accounting and operational workflows.
- **Fraud Monitoring Systems**: GenAI models integrated with transaction monitoring tools provide real-time anomaly detection, flagging potentially fraudulent activities and mitigating risks efficiently.
- **Loan Underwriting:** Integrating GenAI with loan origination systems can expedite the underwriting process by analyzing customer credit profiles, employment histories, and market conditions. AI models can offer risk assessments with high precision, improving loan approval turnaround times.
- **Customer Onboarding:** GenAI-powered identity verification systems integrated into customer onboarding platforms can automate document verification, perform real-time KYC (Know Your Customer) checks, and reduce onboarding times significantly.

Effective integration requires robust **Application Programming Interfaces (APIs)** that ensure seamless communication between GenAI systems and existing tools. Middleware solutions and cloud-based platforms also play a crucial role in maintaining data flow and scalability.

Technical Trends Influencing Finance

Rick Abbott

The rapid advancement of GenAI is driving several critical trends in the finance and banking industry. These innovations are shaping the sector's evolution and opening new opportunities for growth:

- **AI-Powered Fraud Detection**: Advanced algorithms analyze transaction patterns in real time, identifying anomalies that could indicate fraudulent activity. This trend enhances financial security while minimizing manual oversight.
- **Predictive Analytics for Risk Management**: AI systems leverage historical data and real-time inputs to forecast risks, from market fluctuations to credit defaults. These insights enable proactive strategies and better resource allocation.
- **Personalized Chatbots and Virtual Assistants**: GenAI-powered virtual assistants improve customer service by delivering personalized responses, financial advice, and automated support round the clock.
- **Synthetic Data for Model Testing**: Generative models create synthetic datasets for testing risk scenarios, ensuring robust AI performance while maintaining compliance with data privacy regulations.
- **Explainable AI (XAI)**: With growing emphasis on transparency, financial institutions are adopting XAI tools to clarify the decision-making processes behind AI recommendations, building trust with regulators and customers alike.

GenAI tools and technologies are not only transforming individual workflows but also redefining the strategic capabilities of finance and banking institutions. By integrating these tools into existing systems and leveraging emerging trends, financial organizations can unlock unprecedented levels of efficiency, accuracy, and innovation. The adoption of GenAI ensures that institutions remain agile and competitive in an increasingly dynamic financial landscape.

Challenges and Risks

As GenAI becomes integral to finance and banking, it introduces significant ethical challenges. A primary concern is **algorithmic bias**, where AI systems inadvertently produce discriminatory outcomes due to biased training data. This can affect critical areas such as loan approvals and credit scoring, leading to unfair practices that disproportionately impact certain demographic groups. Financial institutions must ensure their AI systems are trained on diverse and representative datasets to mitigate these risks.

Data privacy is another critical ethical concern. GenAI models often process sensitive customer information, such as transaction histories and personal financial details. Mishandling or unauthorized access to this data can lead to privacy violations, eroding trust and exposing institutions to regulatory penalties. The opaque nature of many GenAI models, often referred to as the "black box problem," challenges transparency. Stakeholders may struggle to understand or trust AI-driven decisions without clear explanations of how outcomes were reached.

Risks of Misuse or Dependency on GenAI

The risks associated with misuse or over-dependency on GenAI are profound. Over-reliance on AI systems could reduce human oversight, increasing the likelihood of errors in high-stakes decision-making. For example, automated credit risk assessments may misclassify applicants if anomalies or unforeseen variables are not addressed by human judgment.

Another risk is AI misuse, such as employing GenAI for manipulative practices, including generating fraudulent financial reports or misleading customer communications. Cybersecurity threats further compound the risks, as malicious actors may exploit vulnerabilities in AI systems to infiltrate financial networks or manipulate sensitive data. Dependency on AI also poses operational risks; a system failure or inaccurate model predictions could disrupt key processes, leading to financial losses or reputational damage.

Frameworks to Address Risks

To navigate these challenges and mitigate risks, financial institutions must adopt robust governance frameworks and proactive strategies. Below are five key approaches:

- **Ethical AI Governance**: Establish governance committees to oversee the ethical deployment of GenAI. These committees should focus on fairness, inclusivity, and accountability in AI applications.
- **Data Privacy Regulations**: Adhere strictly to regulations such as GDPR **and** CCPA, ensuring robust encryption,

secure storage, and controlled access to sensitive customer data.

- **AI Bias Mitigation**: Conduct regular audits to identify and address biases in AI models. Leveraging diverse datasets and implementing fairness testing protocols help promote equitable outcomes.

- **Human Oversight in AI Decisions**: Maintain a "human-in-the-loop" system for critical decision-making processes, ensuring that AI-generated insights are reviewed and validated by human experts.

- **Continuous Monitoring and Updates**: Implement systems for real-time monitoring of AI performance and ensure models are regularly updated to address new risks, regulatory changes, or market dynamics.

While GenAI offers transformative opportunities in finance, it also brings ethical, operational, and cybersecurity risks that must be addressed comprehensively. By adopting governance frameworks, maintaining transparency, and ensuring human oversight, financial institutions can leverage GenAI responsibly and effectively. These proactive measures will foster trust, mitigate risks, and ensure that AI-driven innovations align with ethical and regulatory standards, securing long-term success in the evolving financial landscape.

Skillset Evolution

The adoption of GenAI is reshaping the skillsets required in the finance and banking industry, pushing professionals to blend traditional expertise with advanced technical proficiency. Core competencies like financial analysis and risk management must now be complemented by AI literacy, data analytics, and machine learning basics. Finance professionals are increasingly expected to understand how GenAI models generate insights, enabling them to interpret and apply these outputs effectively in areas like fraud detection, credit scoring, and customer engagement.

The demand for soft skills **is** also evolving. Strategic thinking, adaptability, and ethical decision-making are critical as finance teams navigate the complexities of AI-driven systems. Professionals must learn to collaborate with AI tools, maintaining oversight while leveraging their capabilities to enhance efficiency and innovation. Emotional intelligence and communication skills remain vital for translating AI-generated insights into actionable strategies that align with organizational goals.

Training and Upskilling Needs

To meet these new demands, organizations must prioritize comprehensive training and upskilling programs. Employees need foundational knowledge in GenAI concepts, such as how models are trained, their limitations, and their applications in finance. Training programs should include modules on data handling, algorithmic transparency, and ethical considerations to ensure responsible AI use.

Targeted upskilling initiatives should focus on specific tools and technologies. For instance, professionals working in customer engagement can benefit from learning how to deploy and refine AI-powered chatbots, while risk managers should develop expertise in AI-driven predictive analytics. Practical, hands-on experience with GenAI tools like OpenAI's GPT or IBM Watson is essential for building confidence and capability.

Continuous education is equally important. AI technologies evolve rapidly, and organizations must provide access to certifications, workshops, and e-learning platforms to keep teams updated. Partnering with industry experts or academic institutions can further enrich these learning programs, ensuring employees remain competitive and skilled in leveraging AI for financial innovation.

Emerging Roles and Career Paths

The integration of GenAI is also creating new roles in finance, reflecting the industry's growing reliance on AI technologies. These roles blend technical and financial expertise to maximize the benefits of AI-driven solutions. Below are five key emerging roles:

- **AI Compliance Officer**: Ensures adherence to regulatory and ethical standards in AI implementations. Responsibilities include auditing AI systems, addressing biases, and safeguarding customer data privacy.
- **AI-Driven Risk Analyst**: Specializes in using predictive analytics to identify and mitigate risks, such as market volatility, credit defaults, or fraud. These professionals interpret AI outputs to make data-informed decisions.
- **Customer Experience Personalization Expert**: Leverages GenAI to create tailored banking solutions, enhancing customer engagement and loyalty through AI-powered insights.

- **AI Integration Specialist**: Focuses on embedding GenAI tools into existing financial systems, ensuring seamless functionality, scalability, and alignment with organizational goals.
- **Ethical AI Strategist**: Develops frameworks for fair, transparent, and accountable use of AI in finance, addressing concerns such as algorithmic bias and regulatory compliance.

The rise of GenAI is transforming the finance workforce, requiring professionals to develop hybrid skillsets that combine financial acumen with AI proficiency. By investing in targeted training and embracing new career opportunities, organizations can equip their teams to navigate this technological shift effectively. These efforts not only ensure smoother adoption of AI solutions but also position finance professionals to drive innovation and strategic growth in an AI-powered future.

Emerging Trends

GenAI is poised to fundamentally reshape the finance and banking industry over the coming years. As institutions increasingly rely on AI to streamline operations, deliver personalized customer experiences, and enhance risk management, the role of finance professionals will evolve. GenAI's ability to process vast datasets in real time and generate actionable insights will enable institutions to make more informed decisions, optimize resources, and remain competitive in a rapidly changing market. Its long-term impact will be seen in areas such as fraud prevention, dynamic customer service, and compliance with evolving regulatory standards.

Emerging Trends and Their Potential Influence

The financial industry is rapidly evolving, driven by advancements in GenAI and its ability to address complex challenges and opportunities. From enabling real-time decision-making to integrating with decentralized finance platforms and blockchain technology, GenAI is reshaping traditional financial processes and customer interactions. Emerging trends such as AI-driven customer analytics and digital twin finance systems are empowering institutions to provide hyper-personalized services and simulate strategic scenarios with minimal risk. Moreover, the evolution of ethical AI, with a focus on transparency and explainability, is fostering trust and regulatory compliance, ensuring responsible adoption of these transformative technologies. These trends are not only redefining the competitive landscape but also setting new benchmarks for innovation and operational efficiency in the financial sector.

- **Real-Time Decisioning**: GenAI's capacity to analyze data instantaneously enables institutions to make real-time decisions on lending, investments, and fraud detection. This accelerates operations and improves customer satisfaction by providing immediate, accurate solutions.
- **Decentralized Finance (DeFi) and Blockchain Integration**: GenAI simplifies complex blockchain systems, offering predictive analytics for decentralized financial platforms. This trend improves transparency, reduces costs, and expands access to financial services.
- **AI-Driven Customer Analytics**: Leveraging GenAI to analyze customer behavior provides deeper insights into preferences, enabling institutions to offer hyper-personalized products and services.
- **Digital Twin Finance Systems**: Virtual models of financial processes simulate real-time scenarios, allowing institutions to test strategies, predict outcomes, and improve decision-making with minimal risk.
- **Ethical AI Evolution**: With regulators and customers demanding transparency, institutions are adopting Explainable AI (XAI) to clarify how decisions are made, building trust and compliance with ethical standards.

Strategic Priorities for Organizations to Stay Competitive

As GenAI continues to transform the financial landscape, organizations must adopt strategic priorities to maintain a competitive edge while fostering innovation and trust. By investing in ethical AI practices, businesses can ensure compliance with data privacy regulations and build models that emphasize fairness and transparency. Enhancing AI-driven customer solutions is critical to delivering personalized, real-time experiences that drive loyalty and satisfaction. At the same time, strengthening cybersecurity measures is essential to safeguard against the growing risks of cyber threats and AI misuse. Building AI-ready teams through training and upskilling ensures that employees can effectively leverage these technologies, while proactive collaboration with regulators helps shape governance frameworks that balance innovation with compliance. Together, these priorities enable organizations to thrive in an increasingly AI-driven world.

- **Invest in Ethical AI Practices**: Prioritize the development and adoption of GenAI models that emphasize fairness, transparency, and compliance with data privacy regulations.
- **Enhance AI-Driven Customer Solutions**: Focus on creating personalized, real-time experiences that cater to individual customer needs, fostering loyalty and satisfaction.
- **Strengthen Cybersecurity Measures**: As AI becomes integral to finance, robust protections against cyber threats and AI model misuse are essential.
- **Build AI-Ready Teams**: Invest in training programs to develop workforce proficiency in AI tools and applications, ensuring employees can adapt to and optimize new technologies.
- **Foster Regulatory Collaboration**: Work proactively with regulators to shape AI governance frameworks that balance innovation with compliance, ensuring sustainable growth.

GenAI is not only transforming how financial institutions operate today but is also shaping the future of the industry. By embracing emerging trends such as real-time decision-making, blockchain integration, and ethical AI practices, organizations can position themselves as leaders in the evolving financial landscape. Strategic priorities like robust cybersecurity, regulatory collaboration, and workforce readiness will be crucial in harnessing the full potential of GenAI while navigating its complexities. Institutions that proactively adopt and adapt to these trends will gain a significant competitive advantage in the AI-driven future of finance.

Conclusion

GenAI is revolutionizing the finance and banking industry by transforming how institutions manage risk, serve customers, and optimize operations. Its capabilities in real-time fraud detection, predictive analytics, and hyper-personalized customer service are redefining industry standards. GenAI not only streamlines routine tasks but also unlocks innovative approaches to complex challenges, such as regulatory compliance and credit scoring. By integrating AI-driven tools, financial institutions can achieve greater efficiency, improved decision-making, and enhanced customer satisfaction.

The Need for Strategic Thinking and Adaptability

To fully harness the transformative potential of GenAI, financial institutions must approach its adoption with strategic foresight and adaptability. Leaders need to align GenAI initiatives with organizational goals, ensuring that AI solutions address key challenges while driving innovation. This requires investment in robust infrastructure, ethical frameworks, and continuous workforce development to maintain a competitive edge.

As the industry evolves, institutions must also remain agile, adapting to advancements in AI technologies, shifting regulatory landscapes, and changing customer expectations. Collaboration between departments, regulators, and technology providers will be crucial for fostering trust, ensuring compliance, and scaling AI solutions effectively. Organizations must balance automation with human oversight to preserve the critical judgment and creativity that underpin successful financial strategies.

The integration of GenAI into finance and banking is more than a technological upgrade—it is a paradigm shift that demands a proactive and thoughtful approach. Institutions that prioritize innovation, ethical practices, and workforce readiness will not only overcome the challenges posed by AI adoption but also unlock unprecedented opportunities for growth and transformation. By leveraging GenAI responsibly, financial institutions can position themselves as leaders in a rapidly evolving industry, driving both operational excellence and customer value in the AI-powered future of finance.

Key Takeaways

1. **Transforming Risk Management and Fraud Detection**: GenAI enhances risk management by detecting fraudulent activities in real time, analyzing patterns across vast datasets, and enabling proactive prevention. Its ability to continuously learn and adapt ensures institutions remain vigilant against evolving threats, safeguarding assets and trust.

2. **Revolutionizing Customer Experiences**: By leveraging GenAI's ability to analyze customer data, financial institutions can deliver hyper-personalized services, such as tailored financial advice and customized product recommendations. AI-driven chatbots and virtual assistants further enhance engagement, offering instant, 24/7 support.

3. **Streamlining Regulatory Compliance**: GenAI automates complex compliance processes, ensuring adherence to ever-evolving regulations with greater speed and accuracy. By reducing manual errors and operational costs, institutions can

focus more on strategic initiatives while maintaining regulatory integrity.

4. **Evolving Workforce Skillsets**: The integration of GenAI necessitates a workforce proficient in AI literacy, data analytics, and strategic decision-making. Training programs and upskilling initiatives are critical to equip employees with the tools to effectively collaborate with AI systems and unlock innovation.

5. **The Importance of Ethical AI Practices**: As AI becomes central to finance, institutions must prioritize transparency, fairness, and accountability in GenAI applications. Robust ethical frameworks and human oversight are essential to mitigate biases, build trust, and ensure compliance with regulatory and societal expectations.

Financial institutions must embrace GenAI as a transformative force that redefines how they manage risks, serve customers, and drive innovation. By focusing on strategic implementation, continuous learning, and ethical practices, organizations can lead the industry in delivering unparalleled value and resilience in an AI-driven future.

CHAPTER 8: RETAIL AND E-COMMERCE

Introduction to GenAI in Retail and E-Commerce

Retail and e-commerce stand at the forefront of consumer innovation, driving global economic growth and shaping the way people shop, engage with brands, and experience products. This sector is not only a hub for customer interaction but also a testing ground for adopting cutting-edge technologies. As customer expectations evolve rapidly—demanding convenience, personalization, and seamless omnichannel experiences—retailers and e-commerce platforms face mounting pressure to stay ahead of the curve.

GenAI is revolutionizing retail and e-commerce by offering a suite of tools that enhance personalization, streamline operations, and elevate customer engagement. Unlike traditional AI applications that rely on historical patterns to provide insights, GenAI actively creates—

whether through generating personalized product recommendations, crafting marketing content, or optimizing supply chain strategies. Its ability to predict consumer preferences, automate routine tasks, and provide tailored shopping experiences has positioned GenAI as a transformative force in the industry.

Despite these advancements, challenges persist. Retailers often struggle with fragmented customer data, inefficiencies in inventory management, and the increasing complexity of catering to diverse customer needs. Traditional approaches frequently fall short in providing the level of personalization customers now expect, while operational inefficiencies result in lost revenue and lower customer satisfaction. GenAI addresses these gaps by leveraging advanced machine learning models to predict demand, recommend products with pinpoint accuracy, and even generate dynamic content that resonates with individual consumers.

In this chapter, we will explore how GenAI is reshaping retail and e-commerce, delivering personalized experiences at scale, optimizing inventory management, and enhancing customer engagement. By examining the transformative impact of this technology, we aim to uncover the opportunities it presents and the challenges organizations must navigate to succeed in this dynamic, AI-driven landscape.

Transformational Impact

GenAI is profoundly reshaping the retail and e-commerce landscape, driving a shift from broad, generalized strategies to hyper-personalized, data-driven approaches. By leveraging the vast volumes of data generated through digital platforms, GenAI enables businesses to deliver tailored shopping experiences, anticipate consumer needs, and refine their operational workflows. The result is a dynamic transformation in how retailers engage with customers, manage inventory, and streamline decision-making processes.

One of the most significant impacts of GenAI is its ability to provide hyper-personalized customer experiences at scale. Retailers can now analyze real-time behavioral data to generate individualized product recommendations, create dynamic email campaigns, and design targeted advertisements that resonate deeply with each customer. Virtual assistants powered by GenAI further enhance this personalization by assisting customers with tailored suggestions, resolving queries, and guiding them through their shopping journey.

The outcome is a more engaging and satisfying customer experience that fosters loyalty and drives higher conversion rates.

Revolutionizing Retail Operations with GenAI

GenAI is also transforming the operational backbone of retail and e-commerce. Inventory management, a long-standing challenge for businesses, has been revolutionized through predictive analytics. GenAI models analyze historical sales data, seasonal trends, and external factors like weather or economic conditions to accurately forecast demand. This allows retailers to optimize stock levels, reduce waste, and minimize stockouts or overstocking scenarios. Additionally, supply chain processes are becoming more efficient as GenAI identifies potential bottlenecks, recommends logistics adjustments, and automates routine administrative tasks.

Decision-making workflows in retail are evolving with the integration of GenAI tools. Traditionally, retail teams relied on manual data analysis and intuition to shape strategies. Now, GenAI-powered dashboards and insights provide real-time, actionable recommendations, empowering teams to make informed decisions quickly. Whether optimizing product pricing, analyzing market trends, or predicting customer churn, GenAI enhances both the speed and accuracy of strategic planning. This shift fosters greater collaboration across teams, as data and insights are shared seamlessly between marketing, operations, and sales functions.

Top Opportunities for GenAI in Retail and E-Commerce

With the adoption of GenAI, the priorities of retail and e-commerce businesses are also shifting. The focus has moved from merely maximizing sales to creating sustainable, customer-centric models that balance profitability with long-term loyalty. The ability to respond in real time to customer preferences, market fluctuations, and operational challenges positions GenAI as a critical driver of competitive advantage.

- **Hyper-Personalized Shopping Experiences**: GenAI empowers retailers to deliver individually tailored recommendations and promotions based on consumer behavior and preferences. This enhances customer satisfaction and boosts revenue through higher conversion rates.

- **Optimized Inventory Management**: Predictive analytics tools forecast demand with precision, ensuring that stock levels align with market needs. This reduces waste, cuts costs, and improves operational efficiency.
- **Automated Content Creation**: GenAI generates dynamic product descriptions, social media posts, and email campaigns, enabling marketing teams to scale their content strategies while maintaining quality and relevance.
- **Enhanced Customer Service**: AI-driven virtual assistants handle common queries, assist in product selection, and resolve issues, reducing response times and improving the overall customer experience.
- **Dynamic Pricing Strategies**: GenAI analyzes market trends, competitor pricing, and consumer demand to recommend optimal pricing strategies, ensuring competitiveness and profitability.

GenAI is not only enhancing how retailers interact with customers but also redefining the operational and strategic pillars of retail and e-commerce businesses. By automating routine processes, providing actionable insights, and enabling real-time adaptability, GenAI allows companies to navigate the complexities of modern retail with agility and precision. As businesses continue to embrace this technology, they are better positioned to foster deeper customer loyalty, achieve operational excellence, and secure a competitive edge in an ever-evolving marketplace.

Key Technologies and Tools

The integration of GenAI into retail and e-commerce has introduced a host of powerful technologies and tools that enhance customer experiences, streamline operations, and optimize business outcomes. These tools, ranging from advanced machine learning models to sophisticated platforms, enable retailers to leverage data and creativity in unprecedented ways.

Relevant GenAI Models and Platforms

At the forefront of retail transformation are cutting-edge GenAI models such as OpenAI's GPT (Generative Pre-trained Transformer) series, which power intelligent chatbots, personalized recommendations, and dynamic content generation. These models analyze customer behavior and preferences to create highly targeted interactions, whether through virtual shopping assistants or personalized email campaigns. DALL·E, another groundbreaking AI tool, generates compelling visual content, such as product images or promotional materials, tailored to specific marketing needs. Platforms like Google's Bard and IBM Watson provide additional AI capabilities, including natural language understanding and predictive analytics, to support decision-making across retail operations.

Integration with Existing Technologies and Systems

For GenAI to deliver its full potential, seamless integration with existing retail technologies is essential. Many retailers already rely on robust Customer Relationship Management (CRM) platforms like Salesforce or HubSpot to manage customer interactions. GenAI tools can integrate with these systems to provide advanced analytics, automate routine tasks like lead scoring, and generate personalized customer communication. Connecting GenAI with inventory management software such as SAP or Oracle NetSuite allows for real-time demand forecasting and inventory optimization, ensuring that retailers maintain the right stock levels to meet customer needs.

Another key area of integration is with marketing automation tools like Mailchimp or Adobe Campaign. GenAI can enhance these platforms by generating personalized marketing materials, A/B testing content variations, and analyzing campaign performance for real-time adjustments. Middleware solutions and APIs facilitate this integration, enabling data flow between GenAI models and existing systems without disrupting operations.

Technical Trends Influencing Retail

GenAI is at the center of several technological trends shaping the future of retail and e-commerce. These trends are driving innovation and enabling businesses to stay competitive in a rapidly evolving market:

- **Omnichannel Personalization**: GenAI powers consistent and tailored customer experiences across all touchpoints, from in-store interactions to online platforms, ensuring seamless transitions between channels.
- **Visual Search and Recognition**: Advanced AI tools enable customers to search for products using images, making shopping more intuitive and reducing friction in the customer journey.

- **Voice and Conversational AI**: AI-driven voice assistants and chatbots provide real-time support, guiding customers through product selections and troubleshooting issues.
- **Sustainability-Driven Solutions**: GenAI helps retailers optimize supply chains, minimize waste, and track sustainability metrics, aligning with growing consumer demand for environmentally responsible practices.
- **Real-Time Analytics**: GenAI enables businesses to monitor sales trends, customer behavior, and inventory performance through advanced dashboards, facilitating agile decision-making.

By integrating these technologies and staying aligned with emerging trends, retailers and e-commerce businesses can unlock the full potential of GenAI. The ability to deliver personalized customer experiences, optimize operations, and innovate rapidly positions GenAI as a cornerstone of modern retail strategy. As the technology evolves, its applications will continue to expand, reshaping how retailers connect with customers and drive business success.

Challenges and Risks

While GenAI offers transformative opportunities for retail and e-commerce, its adoption also comes with significant challenges and risks. Addressing these hurdles is critical to ensuring ethical use, operational stability, and sustained value creation.

Ethical Challenges

One of the primary ethical concerns in deploying GenAI is maintaining data privacy and security. Retailers collect vast amounts of sensitive customer information, including purchase history, preferences, and personal details. Improper handling of this data or insufficient compliance with regulations like GDPR (General Data Protection Regulation) or CCPA (California Consumer Privacy Act) can result in breaches of trust, legal repercussions, and reputational damage.

Bias in AI models presents another ethical challenge. GenAI systems learn from historical data, which can include inherent biases that may lead to discriminatory recommendations or unfair pricing strategies. For example, a biased algorithm might prioritize certain customer demographics while inadvertently marginalizing others. Ensuring fairness and inclusivity in AI-driven decision-making requires vigilant monitoring and diverse datasets.

Transparency is also a pressing concern. Customers may not always realize that their interactions are AI-driven, leading to potential feelings of deception or mistrust. Clear communication about the role of GenAI in customer interactions is essential to maintaining transparency and building long-term trust.

Risks of Misuse or Overdependence

The risks of over-reliance on GenAI in retail operations can be significant. While automation improves efficiency, excessive dependence on AI systems may reduce the human touch in customer interactions, diminishing the personalized experience that many customers value. Additionally, errors in AI-generated recommendations or predictions—such as incorrect product suggestions or flawed demand forecasts—can lead to dissatisfied customers and financial losses.

Operational vulnerabilities also arise from the potential misuse or malfunction of GenAI systems. Cyberattacks targeting AI infrastructure or data breaches could disrupt retail operations and compromise sensitive customer data. The "black box" nature of some GenAI models makes it challenging to understand how decisions are made, complicating error resolution and accountability.

Frameworks to Address Risks

To mitigate these challenges and risks, retailers must adopt structured frameworks and best practices for GenAI implementation. Below are five key approaches:

- **Transparent AI Policies**: Clearly communicate how AI is used in customer interactions, providing users with the choice to opt out of AI-driven processes if desired. Transparency builds trust and ensures ethical engagement.
- **Bias Mitigation Protocols**: Regularly audit AI models for bias and refine algorithms to ensure equitable outcomes. Use diverse training datasets that represent all customer demographics and avoid reinforcing stereotypes.
- **Data Security Measures**: Implement advanced encryption, access controls, and real-time monitoring to protect sensitive

customer data. Regularly review compliance with data privacy laws like GDPR and CCPA.

- **Human Oversight**: Maintain a "human-in-the-loop" approach for critical decisions, ensuring that AI-generated outputs are validated by human experts. This approach balances AI efficiency with human judgment and empathy.
- **Contingency Planning**: Develop robust incident response plans for AI system failures or cyberattacks. Conduct regular simulations to test preparedness and minimize operational disruptions.

While GenAI has the potential to revolutionize retail and e-commerce, its implementation must be approached thoughtfully and responsibly. Ethical considerations, operational risks, and customer trust are central to successful adoption. By prioritizing transparency, fairness, and robust security measures, retailers can harness the power of GenAI while mitigating its risks, ensuring both innovation and sustainability in their operations.

Skillset Evolution

The adoption of GenAI in retail and e-commerce is transforming the skill requirements for professionals across the industry. As AI tools become integral to customer engagement, inventory management, and operational decision-making, businesses must equip their teams with the necessary expertise to harness the technology effectively. This shift emphasizes not only technical competencies but also strategic and creative skills to fully leverage GenAI's potential.

How GenAI Changes Skill Requirements

With GenAI automating routine tasks such as data analysis, product descriptions, and demand forecasting, professionals in retail must shift their focus to interpreting AI-generated insights and using them to make informed decisions. Roles that previously required manual effort now demand a deep understanding of AI systems, including how to configure, monitor, and refine them for specific business needs. For example, marketing professionals must learn to use AI tools to generate personalized campaigns, while inventory managers must understand predictive analytics to optimize stock levels.

Beyond technical expertise, soft skills such as adaptability, collaboration, and creative problem-solving are becoming increasingly important. GenAI provides the tools, but human oversight ensures that AI-driven strategies align with business objectives and customer expectations.

Training and Upskilling Needs

To prepare for this evolution, businesses must prioritize training and upskilling initiatives that align with the demands of a GenAI-driven environment. Structured learning programs should cover the following areas:

- **AI Fundamentals**: Employees must understand the basics of AI, including how GenAI systems function, their capabilities, and their limitations. This foundational knowledge is crucial for effective collaboration with AI tools.
- **Data Literacy**: Professionals need to learn how to interpret and analyze data to extract actionable insights from GenAI outputs. Training in tools like dashboards and analytics platforms can enhance data-driven decision-making.
- **Ethical AI Practices**: As ethical considerations become more critical, employees should be trained on AI ethics, including bias mitigation, data privacy compliance, and transparency in AI-driven processes.
- **Role-Specific Applications**: Tailored programs should focus on how GenAI can be applied within specific roles. For instance, marketing teams might learn to use AI for content creation and customer segmentation, while operations teams focus on supply chain optimization.
- **Creative Collaboration**: Employees must develop the ability to combine human creativity with AI-generated outputs. This includes enhancing customer experiences, innovating product offerings, and refining marketing strategies.

Emerging Roles in Retail and E-Commerce

The rise of GenAI is creating new roles that require a blend of technical expertise and industry knowledge. These roles highlight the evolving landscape of retail and the growing importance of AI fluency:

- **AI Personalization Strategist**: Focuses on designing customer experiences using AI insights. These professionals leverage data to create hyper-personalized shopping journeys and targeted marketing campaigns.

- **Visual AI Specialist**: Utilizes tools like DALL·E to enhance product images, design virtual try-ons, and create immersive shopping experiences.
- **AI Compliance Officer**: Ensures that GenAI applications in retail adhere to ethical guidelines, data privacy regulations, and transparency standards.
- **Sustainability Analyst**: Uses GenAI to optimize eco-friendly practices in supply chains, including reducing waste and analyzing carbon footprints.
- **Real-Time Analytics Manager**: Oversees AI-driven dashboards to monitor sales, inventory, and customer trends, enabling agile and responsive decision-making.

The integration of GenAI into retail and e-commerce is not just a technological shift but a workforce transformation. By equipping employees with the necessary skills to collaborate effectively with AI systems, businesses can unlock the full potential of GenAI while fostering a culture of innovation and adaptability. As roles evolve and new opportunities emerge, organizations that prioritize upskilling will gain a competitive edge, ensuring they remain agile and customer-focused in an increasingly AI-driven landscape.

Emerging Trends

GenAI is driving transformative trends in retail and e-commerce, reshaping how businesses engage with customers, optimize operations, and strategize for the future. As the technology matures, its influence extends beyond current applications, heralding a new era of personalization, efficiency, and innovation. Understanding these trends is essential for businesses looking to remain competitive in a rapidly evolving industry.

Emerging Trends and Their Potential Influence

Over the next decade, GenAI is expected to redefine retail by enabling hyper-personalized customer experiences, automating complex workflows, and driving sustainability initiatives. The ability to combine real-time data analysis with creative content generation positions GenAI as a cornerstone of modern retail strategies. Retailers and e-commerce platforms that adopt these technologies will gain the agility needed to anticipate market trends, respond to consumer demands, and innovate at scale.

- **Hyper-Personalized Customer Experiences**: GenAI tools are advancing the ability to deliver deeply customized shopping journeys. From AI-driven recommendations to tailored marketing campaigns, personalization will extend beyond online platforms to in-store experiences through augmented reality (AR) and Internet of Things (IoT) integrations. This fosters stronger customer loyalty and higher conversion rates.

- **Real-Time Analytics and Predictive Decision-Making**: GenAI-powered analytics provide actionable insights by analyzing consumer behavior, inventory levels, and market trends in real time. Retailers can make proactive decisions about pricing, stock replenishment, and promotional strategies, enabling them to adapt quickly to changing conditions.

- **Seamless Omnichannel Integration**: GenAI is breaking down barriers between physical and digital retail channels. AI-driven tools ensure consistent customer experiences across websites, mobile apps, social media, and physical stores, offering seamless transitions between touchpoints and improving customer satisfaction.

- **Sustainability and Ethical AI Use**: Consumers increasingly value eco-friendly practices. GenAI tools analyze supply chain data to optimize resource usage, reduce waste, and track carbon footprints. Moreover, businesses are focusing on ethical AI practices, such as bias-free algorithms and transparent data use, to build consumer trust.

- **Voice and Visual Commerce**: GenAI is revolutionizing the way customers search and shop. Voice assistants enable conversational shopping experiences, while visual search tools allow customers to upload images and find matching products effortlessly. These technologies enhance convenience and accessibility.

Strategic Priorities for Staying Competitive

To capitalize on these emerging trends, organizations must adopt strategic priorities that align with the capabilities of GenAI and meet evolving market demands:

- **Invest in Advanced Analytics Platforms**: Retailers should adopt AI-powered platforms that offer real-time insights into consumer behavior, inventory management, and market trends. Advanced analytics enable businesses to make data-driven decisions and maintain a competitive edge.

- **Foster Omnichannel Excellence**: Seamless integration of online and offline channels is critical. Businesses must ensure that their GenAI tools support consistent customer experiences across all touchpoints, from digital storefronts to in-store interactions.
- **Enhance Personalization Capabilities**: Leveraging GenAI's ability to analyze individual customer preferences, businesses can deliver hyper-targeted promotions, recommendations, and content. This not only improves engagement but also boosts sales and loyalty.
- **Prioritize Ethical AI Implementation**: Transparency and fairness in AI applications are essential to building consumer trust. Businesses must establish guidelines for data privacy, bias mitigation, and ethical AI practices to ensure responsible adoption.
- **Drive Sustainability Efforts**: By using GenAI to optimize supply chains, reduce waste, and adopt eco-friendly practices, retailers can meet consumer demand for sustainability while aligning with broader corporate social responsibility goals.

GenAI is revolutionizing retail and e-commerce, introducing trends that promise to reshape the industry for years to come. From hyper-personalization and real-time analytics to omnichannel integration and sustainability, these advancements are driving the future of customer engagement and operational excellence. By adopting forward-looking strategies and aligning with these trends, businesses can harness GenAI's potential to create innovative, ethical, and sustainable retail ecosystems that meet the demands of a dynamic marketplace.

Conclusion

GenAI is transforming the retail and e-commerce landscape by integrating AI-driven tools into every aspect of their operations—from marketing and customer service to inventory management and supply chain optimization—retailers can achieve unprecedented levels of efficiency, innovation, and agility. The era of one-size-fits-all retail is giving way to a new paradigm where data and creativity converge to meet the unique needs of every customer.

To fully capitalize on GenAI's potential, organizations must adopt a forward-thinking approach that aligns technology with strategic objectives. This requires more than just implementing AI tools; it involves fostering a culture of adaptability, collaboration, and ethical responsibility. Retailers must focus on building the necessary infrastructure, upskilling their workforce, and integrating AI into their workflows in a way that enhances both customer experiences and operational outcomes.

Strategic thinking and adaptability are critical as the retail and e-commerce sectors continue to evolve. GenAI is not a static solution but a dynamic enabler of change. Businesses must remain agile, continuously refining their AI-driven strategies to respond to shifts in consumer behavior, emerging trends, and technological advancements. Those who invest in innovation, prioritize ethical practices, and embrace a customer-centric approach will not only stay ahead of the competition but also redefine the future of retail.

As we navigate this transformative era, one thing is clear: the integration of GenAI into retail and e-commerce is more than a technological advancement—it's a new way of thinking about business. By leveraging the power of AI, organizations can unlock opportunities to connect with customers, streamline operations, and create value at a scale that was previously unimaginable. This is the frontier of personalized, efficient, and sustainable retail—a future shaped by GenAI and the businesses bold enough to embrace it.

Key Takeaways

1. **Hyper-Personalization at Scale**: GenAI empowers retailers to deliver deeply customized shopping experiences by analyzing customer behavior and preferences in real-time. From personalized recommendations to tailored marketing campaigns, this capability enhances customer satisfaction, boosts loyalty, and drives higher conversion rates.
2. **Operational Efficiency and Inventory Optimization**: By leveraging predictive analytics, GenAI helps businesses optimize inventory levels, forecast demand with accuracy, and reduce waste. This leads to streamlined supply chains, improved stock management, and significant cost savings across operations.
3. **Automated Content Creation and Engagement**: GenAI enables the generation of dynamic product descriptions, promotional materials, and personalized marketing content. By automating these processes, businesses can maintain

quality and relevance while scaling their content strategies to engage diverse audiences.

4. **Ethical AI Practices Build Trust**
    Transparency, fairness, and compliance are critical for the successful integration of GenAI in retail. Addressing concerns like bias, data privacy, and ethical AI usage not only mitigates risks but also fosters trust among customers and stakeholders, ensuring long-term brand loyalty.

5. **Emerging Roles and Skills in Retail**: The rise of GenAI demands new skillsets, such as AI literacy, data interpretation, and creative collaboration with AI tools. Roles like AI Personalization Strategist and Sustainability Analyst are emerging, reshaping the retail workforce and driving innovation across the sector.

The adoption of GenAI is not merely a technological upgrade but a fundamental shift in how retail and e-commerce operate. By embracing innovation, fostering ethical AI practices, and investing in upskilling, businesses can unlock the full potential of GenAI. This proactive approach ensures they remain competitive while building a customer-centric, sustainable, and future-ready retail ecosystem.

CHAPTER 9: MARKETING AND ADVERTISING

Introduction to GenAI in Marketing and Advertising

Marketing and advertising are pivotal in driving brand awareness, customer engagement, and revenue growth. These functions are the lifeblood of businesses, connecting products and services to their intended audiences. In an era dominated by digital transformation and fierce competition, the ability to craft campaigns that resonate deeply with consumers is more critical than ever. Marketing and advertising not only shape consumer perceptions but also influence purchasing decisions and foster long-term brand loyalty.

High-Level Explanation of GenAI's Relevance

GenAI is redefining the marketing and advertising landscape by introducing unprecedented levels of precision, creativity, and efficiency. At its core, GenAI leverages advanced machine learning models to generate text, images, videos, and other forms of content that mimic human creativity. For marketers, this capability opens doors to hyper-personalized campaigns tailored to the unique preferences and behaviors of individual consumers. The ability to create dynamic, targeted content at scale allows businesses to deepen engagement and achieve measurable results.

GenAI excels in optimizing campaign strategies by analyzing vast datasets, predicting consumer trends, and automating routine tasks. Traditional marketing approaches often rely on manual effort and time-intensive processes, limiting scalability and speed. GenAI addresses these limitations by enabling real-time adjustments to campaigns based on performance data, ensuring that marketing efforts remain relevant and impactful. In advertising, AI-driven tools offer advanced targeting capabilities, helping businesses maximize ROI by reaching the right audience at the right time with the right message.

Current Challenges or Gaps GenAI Can Address

Despite advancements in digital tools, marketing and advertising still face significant challenges. Crafting high-quality, personalized content at scale is a persistent hurdle, often constrained by limited resources and creative bandwidth. Marketers struggle to keep up with the demand for fresh, engaging material across multiple platforms. Analyzing consumer data to derive actionable insights is a complex task, requiring both technical expertise and significant time investments. GenAI streamlines these processes, empowering teams to focus on strategic decision-making rather than operational bottlenecks.

Another critical gap lies in campaign adaptability. Consumer preferences and market conditions can shift rapidly, rendering traditional static campaigns ineffective. GenAI introduces agility into marketing and advertising, enabling real-time optimization based on audience interactions and performance metrics. As concerns around data privacy and ethical AI use grow, businesses must navigate these challenges carefully. GenAI offers tools to address these issues by providing transparency in targeting practices and ensuring compliance with regulatory standards. By addressing these pain points, GenAI not only enhances marketing and advertising effectiveness but also helps businesses build trust with their audiences.

Transformational Impact

GenAI is revolutionizing the marketing and advertising industry by introducing capabilities that blend human creativity with machine-driven precision. Traditionally, marketers and advertisers relied on manual processes for content creation, data analysis, and campaign optimization. GenAI has transformed these tasks, enabling the creation of dynamic, personalized content and providing insights that were previously unattainable. This transformation has unlocked new possibilities for engaging audiences, driving conversions, and scaling campaigns more efficiently than ever before.

One of GenAI's most profound impacts is in hyper-personalization. By analyzing customer data, such as purchase history, browsing behavior, and social media activity, GenAI generates content tailored to individual preferences and needs. For example, AI-driven tools can produce unique email copy, dynamic ad creatives, or targeted video content for different audience segments, ensuring that each consumer interaction feels relevant and meaningful. This level of precision fosters stronger emotional connections with audiences, boosting engagement and loyalty.

GenAI also empowers marketers and advertisers to optimize campaigns in real time. AI-driven tools analyze performance metrics, such as click-through rates and conversion rates, as campaigns unfold. Based on these insights, GenAI can suggest or implement adjustments, such as changing headlines, adjusting visuals, or reallocating budgets to more effective channels. This agility ensures that campaigns remain relevant and impactful, even in rapidly changing market conditions.

Changes in Workflows, Decision-Making, and Team Dynamics

The integration of GenAI into marketing and advertising workflows has significantly reshaped how teams operate. Tasks that once required extensive manual effort, such as content creation, keyword optimization, and audience segmentation, are now streamlined through AI-powered automation. This allows teams to shift their focus from operational tasks to strategic initiatives, such as creative brainstorming, brand positioning, and long-term planning.

Decision-making processes have also evolved with the adoption of GenAI. Marketers can now rely on AI-driven predictive analytics to forecast campaign outcomes, assess audience sentiment, and determine the best course of action. These insights reduce the reliance on intuition and allow for more data-informed strategies, increasing the likelihood of achieving campaign objectives. Collaboration between marketing, creative, and data teams has become more dynamic, as AI tools facilitate the sharing of real-time insights and enable faster execution of ideas.

The Shift in Focus or Priorities Due to GenAI Adoption

As GenAI automates routine tasks and enhances analytical capabilities, marketing and advertising priorities are shifting toward innovation, creativity, and customer-centricity. Marketers are now focusing on developing unique brand narratives and exploring untapped channels for engagement, such as AI-generated immersive experiences or interactive ad formats. The emphasis on agility has grown, with teams prioritizing the ability to adapt quickly to consumer behavior changes and market trends.

Ethical considerations have taken center stage as organizations integrate GenAI into their strategies. Marketers are prioritizing transparency in data usage, ensuring that campaigns respect consumer privacy and align with regulatory standards. This shift reflects a broader commitment to building trust with audiences and maintaining brand integrity in an AI-driven landscape.

Top Opportunities for Meaningful Impact of GenAI

GenAI offers unparalleled opportunities for marketers to deliver hyper-targeted campaigns, optimize performance, and achieve greater ROI. By combining creativity with advanced analytics, GenAI is reshaping the marketing and advertising industry into a more agile, data-driven, and customer-focused domain.

- **Hyper-Personalization:** GenAI enables the creation of campaigns tailored to individual consumer preferences and behaviors. From personalized product recommendations to custom ad creatives, this approach drives deeper engagement and higher conversion rates.
- **Dynamic Content Creation:** With GenAI, marketers can generate large volumes of high-quality content quickly. AI-driven tools produce everything from blog posts and social media captions to videos and interactive media, reducing time-to-market and resource strain.

- **Predictive Campaign Analytics:** GenAI excels in analyzing historical and real-time data to forecast campaign outcomes. This allows marketers to allocate budgets more effectively, predict customer responses, and refine strategies for maximum impact.
- **Cost-Efficiency in Ad Placements:** AI-powered ad targeting ensures that campaigns reach the most relevant audiences, minimizing wasted spend. GenAI analyzes audience behaviors and platform dynamics to optimize placements, enhancing ROI.
- **Real-Time Campaign Adjustments:** GenAI enables dynamic optimization of campaigns based on live feedback. Whether it's altering ad creatives, adjusting targeting criteria, or reallocating budgets, this capability ensures campaigns stay effective throughout their lifecycle.

GenAI is more than a tool—it's a catalyst for transformation in marketing and advertising. By automating processes, delivering actionable insights, and enhancing creativity, GenAI empowers marketers to achieve unparalleled levels of efficiency and engagement. As businesses continue to adopt these technologies, the industry is poised to evolve into a more agile, innovative, and consumer-centric ecosystem.

Key Technologies and Tools

GenAI technologies have introduced a suite of powerful tools tailored to meet the diverse needs of marketers and advertisers. Models like OpenAI's GPT-4, Google's Bard, and Meta's LLaMA provide advanced natural language processing capabilities, enabling the generation of personalized, contextually relevant content for emails, advertisements, and social media posts. Similarly, platforms like Adobe Firefly and DALL·E offer cutting-edge text-to-image generation for creating visuals that align with specific campaign requirements. These technologies help marketers automate content creation, streamline workflows, and enhance customer engagement, ensuring scalability and efficiency.

For analyzing campaign data and optimizing performance, predictive analytics platforms such as Salesforce Einstein and HubSpot's AI tools integrate seamlessly with existing customer relationship management (CRM) systems. These tools provide actionable insights, enabling marketers to refine strategies, allocate budgets effectively, and maximize ROI. Additionally, Dynamic Creative Optimization (DCO) platforms, which use AI to adjust ad creatives in real-time, are transforming how brands interact with audiences across digital channels.

Integration with Existing Marketing Tools and Technologies

Integrating GenAI into existing marketing ecosystems requires careful planning to ensure compatibility and maximize value. GenAI platforms often integrate with CRM systems like Salesforce and HubSpot, enabling real-time personalization of campaigns by leveraging customer data. These integrations help marketers automate processes such as email segmentation, lead scoring, and customer journey mapping, ensuring that campaigns are tailored to individual preferences and behaviors.

Content management systems (CMS) such as WordPress and Adobe Experience Manager can also benefit from GenAI integrations. By embedding AI-driven tools into these platforms, marketers can streamline content creation, optimize website copy for SEO, and deliver personalized user experiences. Social media management tools like Hootsuite and Buffer can leverage GenAI to generate engaging posts, schedule campaigns, and analyze audience sentiment, improving overall social media strategies.

Another critical integration point is with programmatic advertising platforms like Google Ads and Meta Ads Manager. GenAI tools can optimize ad targeting by analyzing consumer behavior and identifying the most effective channels, formats, and timing for ad placements. With these integrations, marketers can execute data-driven campaigns that deliver measurable results while minimizing resource expenditure.

Top 5 Technical Trends

The rapid evolution of technology continues to redefine how businesses engage with customers, optimize operations, and create value. GenAI is at the forefront of this transformation, enabling innovative tools and approaches that enhance personalization, interactivity, and efficiency. From advanced personalization engines that deliver individualized customer experiences at scale to AI-enhanced augmented reality (AR) tools that bridge the gap between physical and digital interactions, these trends are reshaping consumer engagement. Natural Language Generation (NLG) tools and

Dynamic Creative Optimization (DCO) platforms are revolutionizing content creation and advertising by providing contextually relevant and dynamic solutions. Additionally, the integration of voice and conversational AI in marketing strategies is unlocking new ways to connect with audiences through tailored, real-time interactions. Together, these technical trends are driving the next wave of innovation across industries.

- **Advanced Personalization Engines:** GenAI-powered personalization tools enable real-time customer journey mapping, delivering individualized experiences at scale. By analyzing customer behaviors, purchase histories, and preferences, these engines create hyper-targeted campaigns that drive higher engagement and conversions.
- **Augmented Reality (AR) Integration:** AI-enhanced AR tools allow brands to create immersive marketing experiences, such as virtual try-ons or interactive product demos. These technologies bridge the gap between physical and digital experiences, increasing consumer interaction and brand loyalty.
- **Natural Language Generation (NLG) Tools:** AI models like GPT-4 and BERT are transforming content creation by generating high-quality, contextually relevant copy for blogs, product descriptions, and ads. NLG tools improve efficiency and ensure consistency in messaging across platforms.
- **Dynamic Creative Optimization (DCO):** DCO platforms leverage AI to adapt ad creatives in real-time based on audience data and contextual factors, such as location or time of day. This ensures that ads remain relevant and engaging throughout their lifecycle, maximizing impact and ROI.
- **Voice and Conversational AI in Ads:** With the rise of voice-activated devices, AI-driven conversational marketing is becoming a powerful tool for engaging audiences. Voice assistants and chatbots are being used to deliver tailored recommendations, answer questions, and drive conversions in real-time.

The integration of these cutting-edge technologies and trends is reshaping the marketing and advertising landscape. By adopting these tools and staying ahead of emerging innovations, businesses can deliver more impactful campaigns, foster deeper connections with audiences, and achieve sustained growth in an increasingly competitive market.

Challenges and Risks

The integration of GenAI into marketing and advertising introduces a range of ethical challenges that must be carefully navigated to maintain consumer trust and brand integrity. One of the primary concerns is the potential for bias in AI-generated content. AI models are trained on vast datasets that may inadvertently reflect societal biases, leading to campaigns that reinforce stereotypes or alienate specific groups. This risk is particularly pronounced in industries such as fashion, beauty, and health, where messaging must be inclusive and culturally sensitive.

Another ethical challenge lies in transparency. Consumers may not always be aware that content they interact with—whether an email, ad, or social media post—has been generated by AI. This lack of disclosure can erode trust, especially if consumers feel misled or manipulated. For example, AI-generated product reviews or testimonials may appear authentic but could violate ethical advertising standards if not clearly identified. Marketers must balance the creative advantages of GenAI with a commitment to transparency and honesty.

Data privacy is another critical concern. GenAI relies heavily on consumer data to generate personalized campaigns, raising questions about how this data is collected, stored, and used. The improper handling of sensitive information, such as purchasing habits or demographic details, could lead to breaches of privacy regulations like GDPR or CCPA. Ensuring ethical data practices is essential to maintaining consumer confidence and avoiding legal repercussions.

Risks of Misuse or Dependency on GenAI

The potential misuse of GenAI tools presents significant risks for marketing and advertising. Without proper oversight, GenAI could be used to create deceptive or manipulative content, such as fake news or overly aggressive ad targeting. These practices not only harm consumers but also damage brand reputation and invite regulatory scrutiny. GenAI's ability to generate realistic but fabricated imagery or text could blur the lines between truth and fiction in advertising, challenging ethical norms.

Over-dependence on GenAI is another risk, as it may lead to a loss of human oversight and creativity in marketing efforts. While GenAI excels at automating tasks and analyzing data, it lacks the emotional intelligence and cultural nuance required for certain aspects of branding and messaging. Marketers who rely too heavily on AI risk losing the human touch that differentiates compelling campaigns from generic ones. Errors in AI-generated content, such as inaccuracies or inappropriate language, can escalate quickly if not caught by human reviewers, resulting in public backlash.

Operational risks also arise from the technical complexity of GenAI tools. System failures, cybersecurity threats, or issues with model accuracy can disrupt campaigns and lead to financial losses. For example, an AI model that misinterprets data trends might recommend ineffective strategies, wasting resources and diminishing ROI. Businesses must balance the benefits of GenAI with robust risk management practices to ensure sustainable and ethical usage.

Frameworks or Guidelines to Address These Risks

To mitigate these risks and ethical concerns, organizations must adopt structured frameworks and guidelines that promote responsible GenAI usage. Below are five key approaches:

- **Transparency in AI-Generated Content:** Clearly disclose when content has been created by AI, especially in scenarios where authenticity is critical, such as customer reviews or social media posts. Transparency builds trust and ensures compliance with advertising standards.
- **Bias Audits for Ad Targeting:** Regularly audit AI models for bias in content creation and ad targeting. By diversifying training datasets and implementing fairness evaluation metrics, marketers can reduce the likelihood of perpetuating stereotypes or exclusionary practices.
- **Robust Data Privacy Protocols:** Implement stringent data governance practices to ensure compliance with privacy regulations. Encryption, anonymization, and clear user consent mechanisms are essential for protecting consumer information.
- **Human Oversight in Campaign Planning:** Maintain a "human-in-the-loop" approach, where marketers review and approve all AI-generated content before publication. This ensures that messaging aligns with brand values and cultural sensitivities while mitigating potential errors.
- **Real-Time Error Detection Mechanisms:** Use AI monitoring tools to detect inaccuracies, inconsistencies, or

harmful content in real time. These mechanisms can flag issues for immediate review, minimizing reputational damage and ensuring campaign integrity.

While GenAI offers transformative potential in marketing and advertising, it is not without challenges. Ethical concerns such as bias, transparency, and data privacy must be addressed to maintain consumer trust and brand reputation. Additionally, organizations must guard against over-reliance on AI and ensure robust risk management practices to mitigate operational vulnerabilities. By adopting clear frameworks and promoting responsible AI usage, marketers can harness the power of GenAI while safeguarding their values and fostering long-term success.

Skillset Evolution

The adoption of GenAI in marketing and advertising is transforming the skills required for success in these fields. Traditional competencies, such as copywriting, graphic design, and media buying, are being augmented—or in some cases replaced—by skills that enable professionals to collaborate effectively with AI-driven tools. While creativity remains a cornerstone of marketing, the ability to harness GenAI to enhance content, analyze data, and optimize campaigns has become essential.

Marketers now need proficiency in AI tools to generate and refine content, conduct predictive analytics, and personalize consumer experiences. Understanding how to prompt AI systems effectively— using techniques like prompt engineering—has emerged as a critical skill for maximizing the value of GenAI. Professionals must also develop technical literacy to interpret AI outputs, identify errors, and ensure campaigns align with brand values and ethical standards. As GenAI takes on more repetitive tasks, marketers are increasingly expected to focus on strategy, storytelling, and human-centric brand-building.

Training and Upskilling Needs for Teams

To meet the evolving demands of GenAI-driven marketing, organizations must invest in comprehensive training and upskilling programs. These initiatives should focus on both technical and soft skills, ensuring that marketing teams can work effectively alongside AI technologies while maintaining the creativity and empathy that resonate with audiences.

- **Technical Training:** Teams need hands-on experience with AI platforms like OpenAI's GPT-4 or Adobe Firefly to understand their capabilities and limitations. Training should cover key concepts such as prompt engineering, data analysis, and content generation workflows. Marketers should also learn how to integrate AI tools with existing systems, such as CRM platforms or social media management tools.

- **AI Ethics and Governance:** Marketers must be educated on the ethical implications of using GenAI, including how to mitigate biases, protect consumer data, and maintain transparency in AI-generated content. This knowledge is crucial for building campaigns that align with regulatory standards and foster consumer trust.

- **Strategic Thinking and Creativity:** As AI handles more operational tasks, marketers need to sharpen their strategic planning and creative ideation skills. Workshops on storytelling, brand strategy, and consumer psychology can help teams craft campaigns that stand out in a competitive landscape.

- **Collaborative Skills:** GenAI adoption often requires cross-functional collaboration between marketing, data science, and IT teams. Marketers should develop communication and project management skills to ensure seamless integration of AI technologies into broader organizational workflows.

- **Continuous Learning:** Given the rapid evolution of GenAI, organizations should offer ongoing training opportunities to keep teams up-to-date on emerging tools, trends, and best practices. Certifications, e-learning platforms, and hackathons can reinforce a culture of innovation and adaptability.

Emerging Roles

The integration of GenAI is creating new career opportunities within marketing and advertising. These roles reflect the increasing importance of AI technologies in shaping campaigns and driving business outcomes. Below are five emerging roles:

- **AI Marketing Strategist:** This role involves leveraging GenAI tools to design data-driven marketing strategies. AI marketing strategists use predictive analytics to identify consumer trends, optimize campaign performance, and align marketing initiatives with business objectives.

- **Creative AI Content Designer:** Specializing in AI-driven content creation, this role focuses on developing visually engaging and contextually relevant assets using tools like DALL·E and Adobe Firefly. These professionals ensure that AI-generated content aligns with brand guidelines and audience expectations.

- **GenAI Campaign Analyst:** This professional monitors the performance of AI-driven campaigns, analyzing real-time data to make adjustments and maximize ROI. Their expertise lies in interpreting AI outputs and identifying actionable insights to enhance campaign effectiveness.

- **Ethical AI Advertising Officer:** This role ensures that GenAI applications adhere to ethical standards and regulatory guidelines. Responsibilities include auditing AI models for bias, ensuring transparency in AI-generated content, and developing policies to maintain consumer trust.

- **Cross-Channel AI Integrator:** This specialist focuses on integrating GenAI tools across multiple marketing platforms, such as CRM systems, social media management tools, and programmatic advertising platforms. Their goal is to ensure consistency and efficiency in AI-driven campaigns across all channels.

The rise of GenAI is reshaping marketing and advertising skillsets, requiring professionals to adapt to a landscape where data-driven decision-making, ethical considerations, and creative innovation coexist. By prioritizing training and embracing emerging roles, organizations can position their marketing teams to thrive in an AI-augmented world. These new skillsets and roles not only enhance campaign efficiency and impact but also empower teams to navigate the complexities of a rapidly evolving industry.

Emerging Trends

The long-term integration of GenAI in marketing and advertising promises to transform the industry into a more personalized, efficient, and data-driven ecosystem. As AI technologies continue to evolve, marketers will increasingly rely on AI to anticipate consumer preferences, deliver tailored experiences, and create dynamic campaigns that adapt to real-time interactions. This shift will not only enhance customer satisfaction but also enable brands to build deeper connections with their audiences.

Over time, GenAI's predictive capabilities will redefine how marketing strategies are planned and executed. AI-powered tools will provide granular insights into consumer behaviors, enabling marketers to identify trends and opportunities before they fully materialize. Furthermore, the fusion of AI with emerging technologies like augmented reality (AR) and virtual reality (VR) will pave the way for immersive and interactive advertising experiences that were previously unimaginable.

Emerging Trends and Their Potential Influence

The adoption of GenAI is giving rise to several transformative trends that are reshaping marketing and advertising:

- **Hyper-Personalized Consumer Experiences:** GenAI's ability to analyze vast amounts of data allows brands to deliver hyper-personalized campaigns at scale. From individualized product recommendations to dynamic email content, marketers can now create experiences that resonate deeply with consumers, driving engagement and loyalty.
- **AI-Generated Immersive Media:** The integration of AI with AR and VR technologies is enabling brands to create immersive marketing experiences. Virtual try-ons, interactive storytelling, and AI-generated 3D environments are becoming powerful tools for engaging consumers in innovative ways.
- **Real-Time Campaign Adaptability:** GenAI is transforming static campaigns into dynamic entities that evolve in real time. AI tools can analyze performance data mid-campaign and adjust creatives, targeting, or messaging, ensuring maximum relevance and impact.
- **Sustainability-Focused Marketing:** As consumers become more environmentally conscious, AI tools are helping brands align their campaigns with sustainability goals. By analyzing carbon footprints, optimizing resource allocation, and promoting sustainable practices, marketers can meet the growing demand for eco-friendly messaging.
- **AI-Driven Content Moderation:** As content volumes grow, GenAI is being used to ensure that advertising remains aligned with ethical standards. AI tools can detect inappropriate or harmful content, safeguarding brand reputation and compliance with advertising regulations.

Rick Abbott
Strategic Priorities for Organizations to Stay Competitive

To leverage these trends effectively, organizations must align their marketing strategies with the opportunities offered by GenAI. Below are the top five strategic priorities for staying competitive in an AI-driven marketing landscape:

- **Adopting Multimodal AI Tools:** Invest in GenAI platforms capable of handling diverse content formats, such as text, images, video, and audio. This enables brands to create cohesive, cross-platform campaigns that resonate with audiences in various channels.
- **Investment in AI-Driven Consumer Insights:** Leverage GenAI's predictive analytics capabilities to gain deeper insights into consumer behavior and preferences. These insights can guide campaign planning, product development, and customer engagement strategies.
- **Balancing Creativity and Automation:** While GenAI excels at automating repetitive tasks, marketers must ensure that human creativity remains at the forefront. A balanced approach combines AI's efficiency with human ingenuity to produce innovative and emotionally resonant campaigns.
- **AI Ethics and Governance in Marketing:** Establish clear ethical guidelines for AI usage to address concerns such as bias, transparency, and data privacy. Proactively managing these issues builds consumer trust and ensures compliance with evolving regulations.
- **Continuous Learning for Marketing Teams:** Foster a culture of continuous learning by upskilling marketing teams in AI tools and emerging technologies. This ensures that professionals remain agile and capable of adapting to new trends and innovations.

The rapid evolution of GenAI is reshaping marketing and advertising into a more dynamic and innovative field. By embracing emerging trends and focusing on strategic priorities such as multimodal content creation, sustainability, and ethical AI practices, organizations can position themselves for long-term success. As brands adapt to this new era, they will not only achieve greater efficiency and impact but also deepen their connections with consumers, fostering loyalty and competitive advantage in an increasingly AI-driven marketplace.

Conclusion

GenAI is revolutionizing the marketing and advertising industry, empowering businesses to create more personalized, engaging, and data-driven campaigns than ever before. By automating routine tasks, generating creative content, and providing actionable insights, GenAI enables marketers to focus on innovation and strategy. From hyper-personalized consumer experiences to dynamic, real-time campaign adjustments, the potential of GenAI to drive efficiency, engagement, and ROI is unparalleled. As organizations embrace these tools, they are reimagining how they connect with audiences and adapt to evolving consumer expectations.

This transformation requires more than the adoption of cutting-edge technology—it demands a strategic approach rooted in adaptability, ethical considerations, and creativity. As GenAI reshapes the industry, businesses must strike a balance between leveraging automation and preserving the human touch that forms the foundation of compelling brand narratives. This includes maintaining transparency in AI-generated content, protecting consumer data, and fostering trust through responsible AI usage.

The rapid evolution of GenAI underscores the importance of strategic thinking and continuous learning. Marketing professionals must not only master AI tools but also remain agile in adapting to new trends and innovations. Organizations that invest in upskilling their teams, integrating GenAI seamlessly into their workflows, and aligning their efforts with ethical guidelines will position themselves as leaders in the AI-driven future of marketing and advertising.

As businesses navigate this transformative era, they can redefine the boundaries of creativity and efficiency. By embracing the potential of GenAI, organizations can unlock unprecedented possibilities for engaging audiences, driving growth, and building lasting connections with their customers. The future of marketing and advertising lies in the thoughtful and innovative application of AI technologies—tools that empower both brands and consumers to thrive in an increasingly interconnected and dynamic digital landscape.

Key Takeaways

1. **GenAI Revolutionizes Campaign Personalization:**
   GenAI enables marketers to deliver hyper-targeted campaigns tailored to individual consumer preferences and

behaviors. By analyzing vast amounts of data, GenAI creates content that resonates deeply with audiences, fostering engagement, loyalty, and higher conversion rates.

2. **Dynamic Optimization Enhances Campaign Performance:** GenAI allows for real-time adjustments to campaigns, ensuring they remain relevant and effective as audience behaviors or market conditions change. This dynamic capability maximizes ROI by continuously optimizing messaging, visuals, and targeting strategies.

3. **Integration of AI Tools Drives Efficiency:** Seamlessly integrating GenAI with existing marketing systems, such as CRMs and social media platforms, streamlines workflows and reduces operational bottlenecks. Marketers can automate repetitive tasks, focus on strategic initiatives, and achieve better results with fewer resources.

4. **Ethical AI Practices Protect Consumer Trust:** Transparency, data privacy, and fairness are critical in leveraging GenAI responsibly. Organizations must adopt robust ethical frameworks to address concerns such as bias and misuse while ensuring compliance with regulations and maintaining audience trust.

5. **Emerging Roles and Skillsets Unlock New Opportunities:** The rise of GenAI is reshaping the marketing workforce, creating demand for roles like AI Marketing Strategists and Creative AI Content Designers. Professionals equipped with a blend of creativity, data literacy, and AI expertise will lead the industry in innovation and growth.

As the marketing and advertising landscape evolves, organizations must view GenAI not just as a tool for efficiency but as a driver of innovation and transformation. By embracing its capabilities thoughtfully and ethically, businesses can unlock new opportunities, stay ahead of the competition, and build lasting connections with their audiences. Now is the time to invest in AI-powered solutions, upskill teams, and reimagine the future of marketing through the limitless potential of GenAI.

CHAPTER 10: ENTERTAINMENT AND MEDIA

Introduction to GenAI in Entertainment and Media

The entertainment and media industry has always been a cornerstone of cultural and economic growth, shaping narratives, inspiring innovation, and connecting audiences worldwide. From blockbuster films and immersive video games to personalized streaming services, this sector thrives on creativity and storytelling, continually evolving to meet the ever-changing demands of a global audience. In today's digital-first world, where technology and content consumption habits are rapidly advancing, the need for innovative tools and strategies to maintain relevance and engagement has never been greater.

GenAI is emerging as a transformative force within this dynamic industry, introducing unprecedented capabilities for content creation, personalization, and collaboration. By leveraging machine learning algorithms to generate text, images, video, and audio, GenAI is revolutionizing traditional workflows and expanding creative possibilities. Writers, directors, game developers, and media producers can now collaborate with AI tools to accelerate production timelines, craft immersive narratives, and deliver hyper-personalized experiences tailored to individual preferences.

The entertainment and media industry faces unique challenges that GenAI is particularly well-suited to address. The demand for high-quality, diverse content often outpaces traditional production methods, leading to strained resources and missed opportunities. Keeping audiences engaged in an era of fragmented attention spans and endless content options requires innovative solutions that go beyond one-size-fits-all approaches. Ethical concerns surrounding intellectual property, bias, and cultural sensitivity add complexity to content creation and distribution.

GenAI offers a way forward, addressing these challenges by automating labor-intensive tasks, generating fresh ideas, and enabling creators to focus on strategic and artistic decisions. As the line between human creativity and AI-driven innovation continues to blur, entertainment and media professionals must navigate this new frontier with both enthusiasm and responsibility. The integration of GenAI into this industry promises not only to enhance creativity and efficiency but also to redefine how stories are told and consumed in the digital age.

Transformational Impact

GenAI is reshaping the entertainment and media industry, unlocking new dimensions of creativity, efficiency, and audience engagement. Traditionally, content creation involved time-consuming processes reliant on human labor, from brainstorming storylines to designing intricate visuals. GenAI now accelerates these workflows by providing tools that can generate scripts, design characters, produce special effects, and even create music, all while maintaining high-quality outputs. By enabling creators to experiment with ideas more freely and iterate faster, GenAI empowers storytellers to focus on crafting compelling narratives that resonate with audiences on a deeper level.

The integration of GenAI is also transforming decision-making and team dynamics across the entertainment landscape. Producers and directors can use AI-driven insights to make data-informed creative choices, from selecting themes and settings to optimizing casting decisions. These insights, derived from audience preferences and consumption patterns, help creators deliver content that is more likely to succeed. Team workflows have become increasingly collaborative, as GenAI tools facilitate seamless communication between creators, editors, and technical teams, reducing bottlenecks and enhancing overall productivity.

Opportunities for Meaningful Impact of GenAI

The adoption of GenAI is driving a shift in priorities for entertainment and media professionals. Instead of focusing solely on time and cost efficiencies, the industry is now emphasizing audience personalization, interactive storytelling, and real-time content adaptability. GenAI-powered tools allow for the creation of highly customized experiences, such as personalized streaming recommendations, dynamic gaming environments, and tailored advertising campaigns. This shift aligns with the growing demand for content that feels uniquely relevant to individual viewers.

- **Enhanced Storytelling**: GenAI tools assist writers and producers in developing complex, multi-dimensional narratives by generating ideas, drafting scripts, and even proposing plot twists. This not only accelerates the creative process but also opens the door to stories that reflect diverse perspectives and cultural experiences.
- **Virtual Production**: GenAI streamlines pre-production by creating digital sets, generating visual concepts, and enabling real-time collaboration between geographically dispersed teams. These capabilities reduce costs and speed up production timelines while enhancing creative freedom.
- **Immersive Experiences**: GenAI powers augmented reality (AR) and virtual reality (VR) platforms by generating interactive and personalized content, such as immersive game environments or virtual concerts. These experiences deepen audience engagement by offering unique, participatory storytelling opportunities.
- **Efficient Post-Production**: Video editing, sound design, and visual effects creation are significantly enhanced by GenAI tools, which automate repetitive tasks while maintaining precision and creativity. This allows post-production teams to focus on refining their artistic vision.

- **Audience Personalization**: GenAI analyzes viewer data to deliver personalized content recommendations, trailers, or even alternate endings tailored to individual preferences. This level of customization fosters stronger audience loyalty and keeps viewers engaged.

GenAI is not merely a tool for streamlining existing processes; it is a catalyst for reimagining how content is created, distributed, and experienced. From empowering creative teams with AI-driven collaboration to transforming how audiences interact with stories, GenAI is revolutionizing the entertainment and media industry. As professionals embrace these technologies, they unlock new opportunities to captivate audiences, drive innovation, and redefine the boundaries of creative expression. This evolution, while exciting, demands a careful balance between leveraging AI's potential and maintaining the authenticity and ethical integrity that audiences value.

Key Technologies and Tools

GenAI is driving a wave of innovation in the entertainment and media industry, powered by advanced tools and platforms that are transforming creative workflows and audience engagement. These technologies are enhancing how content is conceptualized, produced, and distributed, enabling creators to deliver richer experiences with greater efficiency. From AI-generated scripts to real-time audience analytics, the tools available today provide unprecedented opportunities to push creative boundaries while addressing industry challenges.

Overview of Relevant GenAI Models, Platforms, or Tools

Key GenAI models, such as OpenAI's GPT series and DALL·E, have become cornerstones for content creation. GPT models excel in generating dialogue, storylines, and marketing copy, while DALL·E is revolutionizing visual storytelling by producing detailed images from textual prompts. Tools like Adobe Firefly enable creative professionals to generate high-quality graphics and effects tailored to specific needs. In the audio domain, platforms such as AIVA (Artificial Intelligence Virtual Artist) create original soundtracks and scores, while Descript automates audio editing and transcription, enhancing efficiency for podcasters and video creators.

Gaming and interactive media have benefited from tools like Unity's AI-powered content generation and Unreal Engine's AI tools, which help design realistic environments and dynamic characters. For personalized viewer experiences, platforms like Netflix and YouTube leverage AI-driven recommendation algorithms to tailor content suggestions based on individual preferences.

Integration with Existing Technologies or Systems

Integrating GenAI into existing entertainment and media systems requires thoughtful alignment with current workflows. Tools like OpenAI's API enable seamless integration of language and image generation capabilities into production pipelines. For example, integrating GenAI with scriptwriting software allows writers to generate scene ideas or dialogue options, speeding up ideation without disrupting the creative process.

In visual production, GenAI can enhance tools like Adobe Premiere Pro or After Effects by automating repetitive tasks such as color grading and motion tracking, freeing editors to focus on creative refinement. Similarly, incorporating AI into game development engines, such as Unreal Engine or Unity, streamlines world-building processes by automating asset creation and environmental design. For streaming platforms, GenAI can be integrated with recommendation systems to enhance content curation and improve user engagement.

Collaboration tools like Slack or Microsoft Teams also benefit from GenAI integration, enabling teams to brainstorm, plan, and execute creative projects in real-time. AI-powered transcription and summarization features further improve efficiency in virtual production environments, ensuring that distributed teams remain connected and productive.

Technical Trends

- **AI-Driven CGI (Computer-Generated Imagery)**: GenAI is advancing CGI by creating realistic characters, environments, and effects with minimal human intervention. This technology reduces production costs and expands the scope of visual storytelling.
- **Deepfake Innovations**: While controversial, deepfake technology is revolutionizing how actors and digital doubles are used in production. With proper ethical safeguards, this technology allows for creative opportunities like recreating historical figures or enhancing visual effects.

- **Interactive AI Agents**: AI-powered characters and NPCs (non-playable characters) are elevating gaming and interactive storytelling. These agents can adapt to player choices, creating highly personalized and immersive experiences.
- **Real-Time Data Analytics**: Platforms are increasingly using AI to analyze audience feedback and engagement metrics during production and distribution. These insights allow creators to optimize content strategies and ensure relevance.
- **Generative Sound Design**: GenAI is automating sound creation, allowing for the generation of unique audio elements tailored to specific scenes or atmospheres. This technology enables sound designers to craft immersive auditory experiences with greater efficiency.

The integration of GenAI tools and technologies is redefining how entertainment and media professionals create and deliver content. By enhancing existing systems and embracing emerging trends, the industry is positioned to push creative boundaries, optimize workflows, and captivate audiences in new and exciting ways. Success depends on careful integration, ensuring that these tools complement rather than disrupt established creative processes.

Challenges and Risks

While GenAI holds transformative potential for the entertainment and media industry, its adoption is not without challenges. Ethical concerns, data security risks, and over-dependence on AI systems must be carefully managed to ensure responsible and sustainable integration. These issues require a proactive approach to mitigate risks and establish frameworks that foster innovation without compromising trust or creative integrity.

Ethical Challenges in Entertainment and Media

One of the most significant ethical concerns in the entertainment and media industry is the potential misuse of AI-generated content. Deepfake technology, for example, can be used to create realistic but deceptive imagery or video, raising questions about authenticity and trust. GenAI models trained on existing works may inadvertently plagiarize or infringe upon copyrighted material, exposing creators and organizations to legal and reputational risks. Ensuring that AI-generated outputs respect intellectual property rights is critical to maintaining ethical standards in the industry.

Bias in AI-generated content also poses a challenge. If GenAI models are trained on datasets that lack diversity or reflect existing prejudices, the resulting content may perpetuate stereotypes or exclude underrepresented voices. This can have far-reaching implications for inclusivity and representation in media. Addressing these biases requires careful curation of training data and ongoing monitoring of AI outputs to ensure fairness and cultural sensitivity.

Risks of Misuse or Dependency on GenAI

The misuse of GenAI tools could lead to a range of issues, from the creation of inappropriate or offensive content to the erosion of trust in media. For instance, audiences may become skeptical of content authenticity if they suspect over-reliance on AI tools. Over-dependence on GenAI could undermine human creativity, with organizations prioritizing AI efficiency over the unique insights and emotional depth that human creators bring to storytelling.

Technical and operational risks also come into play. AI-generated outputs can sometimes produce unexpected or inaccurate results, particularly in fast-paced production environments where quality and precision are paramount. Over-reliance on AI systems without adequate human oversight can lead to errors that are costly to correct and damaging to a project's reputation.

Frameworks or Guidelines to Address These Risks

To ensure the responsible use of GenAI in entertainment and media, organizations must adopt comprehensive frameworks and guidelines that balance innovation with accountability. Below are five key approaches:

- **Ethical Content Guidelines**: Establish clear standards for the ethical use of GenAI in content creation. These guidelines should address issues like bias mitigation, cultural sensitivity, and the ethical limits of AI-generated visuals or narratives.
- **Copyright Compliance Tools**: Implement systems that track and verify the originality of AI-generated content to safeguard intellectual property and prevent copyright infringement. Legal teams should be actively involved in the development and use of these tools.

- **Transparency Standards**: Communicate openly with audiences about the use of AI in content creation. Transparency builds trust and ensures that consumers are aware of when and how GenAI tools are being employed in media production.
- **Bias Mitigation Protocols**: Regularly audit and refine AI models to identify and eliminate biases in training data. Ensuring that datasets represent diverse perspectives and voices is essential for promoting inclusivity in media.
- **Regulatory Alignment Systems**: Stay informed about emerging regulations surrounding AI use in creative industries. Aligning with global and regional standards ensures compliance and fosters trust among stakeholders.

The integration of GenAI into entertainment and media must be approached with careful consideration of ethical and operational risks. By addressing challenges such as content authenticity, intellectual property concerns, and bias, the industry can unlock the potential of GenAI while maintaining its commitment to creativity, inclusivity, and integrity. With robust frameworks and responsible practices in place, GenAI can become a valuable ally in redefining storytelling and audience engagement.

Skillset Evolution

The adoption of GenAI in the entertainment and media industry is redefining the skills required for professionals across all roles. As AI takes on more responsibilities in content creation, editing, and audience engagement, the workforce must adapt to new demands, balancing technical proficiency with creative expertise. This evolution emphasizes the need for professionals to collaborate with AI tools effectively while maintaining the human touch that makes storytelling and media compelling.

How GenAI Changes the Skill Requirements for Professionals

GenAI automates many routine tasks, such as script drafting, visual effects generation, and audience analytics. As a result, professionals must shift their focus to higher-level functions that involve strategy, critical thinking, and creative oversight. For example, writers and directors may spend less time on manual revisions and more time guiding AI-generated narratives to align with their artistic vision. Similarly, video editors must learn to work with AI-driven editing tools, using them to enhance efficiency while preserving the emotional impact of their work.

Technical skills, such as understanding how GenAI models function, training AI systems, and interpreting AI-generated insights, are becoming essential. Professionals in media production need to be comfortable using AI-powered platforms for tasks like CGI, sound design, and audience engagement. At the same time, soft skills like adaptability, collaboration, and ethical judgment are critical as teams navigate the opportunities and challenges posed by AI integration.

Training and Upskilling Needs

To thrive in a GenAI-driven industry, professionals require targeted training programs that address both technical and creative competencies. Training initiatives should include:

- **AI Literacy Programs**: Professionals must gain a foundational understanding of how GenAI tools operate, including their strengths, limitations, and ethical considerations. AI literacy helps bridge the gap between creative teams and technical specialists, fostering better collaboration.
- **Hands-On Training with GenAI Tools**: Workshops and certifications focused on industry-specific GenAI platforms—such as scriptwriting assistants, visual effects generators, and predictive analytics tools—equip professionals with practical skills.
- **Creative Problem-Solving with AI**: Training should emphasize how to use GenAI as a creative collaborator, encouraging professionals to explore innovative applications of AI tools in storytelling, production, and audience engagement.
- **Data Interpretation and Decision-Making**: Professionals need skills to analyze AI-driven insights, such as audience preferences or content performance metrics, and apply these insights to improve strategies and creative outputs.
- **Ethics and Bias Awareness**: Upskilling programs must address the ethical implications of GenAI, including bias in datasets, intellectual property concerns, and transparency in AI-generated content.

New Roles or Career Paths Emerging in the Industry

The integration of GenAI is creating entirely new roles that blend technical expertise with creative problem-solving. These emerging positions highlight the industry's shift toward AI-driven innovation:

- **AI Content Strategist**: Responsible for designing and managing AI-generated media projects, this role involves aligning GenAI tools with creative goals and audience preferences. AI Content Strategists ensure that AI outputs enhance storytelling and align with brand identity.
- **Virtual Production Manager**: Overseeing the integration of GenAI tools into digital filmmaking processes, this role focuses on using AI for real-time virtual sets, dynamic lighting, and collaborative workflows that enhance production efficiency.
- **Interactive Experience Designer**: Leveraging GenAI to create immersive and personalized storytelling experiences, these professionals design interactive narratives for gaming, virtual reality (VR), and augmented reality (AR) platforms.
- **Digital Rights Analyst**: Tasked with monitoring and managing AI-generated intellectual property (IP), this role ensures compliance with copyright laws and tracks the originality of GenAI-created content.
- **Ethical AI Media Consultant**: Specializing in the responsible use of GenAI in creative workflows, these consultants provide guidance on ethical practices, transparency, and bias mitigation to maintain audience trust.

The skillset evolution driven by GenAI adoption is reshaping the entertainment and media workforce. By combining technical expertise, creative innovation, and ethical judgment, professionals can effectively collaborate with AI tools to push the boundaries of storytelling and audience engagement. Through targeted training programs and the emergence of new roles, the industry is preparing for a future where human creativity and AI capabilities complement each other to deliver transformative content experiences.

Emerging Trends

GenAI is driving transformative trends in the entertainment and media industry, reshaping how content is created, delivered, and experienced. As this technology becomes more sophisticated, its influence on storytelling, production, and audience engagement is accelerating. These emerging trends highlight the growing role of AI in defining the future of creative industries.

Predicted Long-Term Impact of GenAI on the Industry

GenAI will transition from a supportive tool to a central pillar of the entertainment and media ecosystem. AI-driven tools will enable hyper-personalized content, allowing creators to craft unique experiences tailored to individual preferences. Interactive storytelling powered by GenAI will become increasingly immersive, with users shaping narratives in real-time through gaming, virtual reality (VR), or augmented reality (AR) platforms. These advancements will redefine audience expectations, shifting the focus from passive consumption to active participation.

GenAI will play a critical role in streamlining production pipelines. Virtual production, automated editing, and AI-assisted special effects will significantly reduce costs and time-to-market, making high-quality content creation accessible to a broader range of creators. At the same time, GenAI's predictive capabilities will revolutionize audience analytics, enabling creators to anticipate trends, adapt to market demands, and deliver content that resonates with evolving tastes.

Emerging Trends and Their Potential Influence

- **AI-Generated Interactive Storytelling**: GenAI is enabling dynamic, interactive narratives in gaming and VR experiences. Players can influence story outcomes, dialogue, and character behavior, creating deeply engaging and personalized entertainment.
- **Hyper-Personalized Content Experiences**: Streaming platforms and content providers are leveraging GenAI to tailor recommendations, create personalized trailers, and even suggest alternate storylines based on viewer preferences. This trend enhances viewer engagement and loyalty.
- **Synthetic Media and Digital Humans**: GenAI is driving the creation of highly realistic digital humans and synthetic voices, opening opportunities for virtual influencers, immersive storytelling, and cost-effective production. This technology is also transforming how actors and characters are portrayed on screen.
- **AI-Powered Real-Time Production**: Virtual production tools that integrate GenAI allow for real-time adjustments to sets, lighting, and character design, enabling seamless collaboration among geographically dispersed teams. This trend is accelerating the adoption of remote workflows.

- **Ethical AI Governance in Media**: As GenAI adoption grows, there is a rising focus on ethical frameworks to ensure transparency, reduce bias, and address intellectual property concerns. These frameworks are becoming essential for maintaining trust and accountability in AI-generated content.

Strategic Priorities for Organizations to Stay Competitive

To harness the full potential of these trends, organizations must adopt forward-thinking strategies that prioritize innovation, adaptability, and ethical practices. Below are five strategic priorities:

- **Adopting Real-Time AI Tools**: Invest in AI-powered tools for virtual production, interactive storytelling, and real-time analytics to enhance creative workflows and accelerate production timelines.
- **Expanding AR/VR Content Creation**: Leverage GenAI to design immersive experiences that redefine audience engagement. Focus on developing content for gaming, education, and virtual events, where interactive storytelling thrives.
- **Building AI Centers of Excellence**: Establish centralized hubs to drive GenAI innovation across departments. These centers can provide expertise, training, and strategic direction for integrating AI into creative processes.
- **Investing in AI Ethics Training**: Educate teams on the ethical implications of GenAI, including data privacy, intellectual property, and cultural sensitivity. Aligning AI use with audience values builds trust and fosters sustainable adoption.
- **Leveraging Global Talent Through AI Collaboration**: Use GenAI to facilitate global creative collaboration, enabling teams across borders to co-create and innovate seamlessly. AI-driven tools for language translation, real-time editing, and virtual collaboration reduce barriers and foster inclusivity.

The emergence of GenAI is shaping a new era for entertainment and media, marked by interactive storytelling, hyper-personalization, and streamlined production processes. These trends are redefining audience expectations and enabling creators to deliver content that is more engaging, efficient, and innovative. To remain competitive, organizations must embrace these changes strategically, aligning their workflows, technologies, and workforce with the opportunities

GenAI presents. By focusing on adaptability and ethical integration, the industry can navigate this transformative era with confidence and creativity.

Conclusion

GenAI is revolutionizing the entertainment and media industry, offering unprecedented opportunities to enhance creativity, streamline production, and deliver hyper-personalized experiences. By integrating advanced AI tools into workflows, the industry is transforming how stories are told, how content is produced, and how audiences engage. From crafting immersive narratives to automating complex visual effects, GenAI is pushing the boundaries of what is possible in creative expression.

The adoption of GenAI is not without its challenges. Issues such as ethical content creation, intellectual property concerns, and bias in AI-generated outputs demand thoughtful consideration. As the industry embraces these transformative tools, it must balance innovation with responsibility, ensuring that AI enhances creativity without compromising authenticity or cultural integrity. By addressing these challenges proactively, entertainment professionals can foster trust and uphold the values that make storytelling so impactful.

The path forward requires strategic thinking and adaptability. Organizations must align GenAI initiatives with their creative and business objectives, invest in workforce upskilling, and prioritize ethical governance. Success will depend on fostering a culture that embraces collaboration between human creativity and AI capabilities, leveraging the strengths of both to deliver compelling and meaningful content.

As the entertainment and media industry enters this new frontier, the potential of GenAI to redefine storytelling is vast. By harnessing this technology responsibly and creatively, organizations can not only captivate audiences but also lead the way in shaping the future of media. The journey ahead is one of innovation, imagination, and transformation—one where the fusion of human ingenuity and AI-driven possibilities will inspire generations to come.

Key Takeaways

1. **Transforming Storytelling and Creativity**: GenAI is revolutionizing storytelling by assisting in scriptwriting, plot development, and visual effects generation. These tools enable creators to experiment more freely, explore diverse narratives, and produce engaging content faster and more efficiently.

2. **Streamlining Production Processes**: GenAI-powered tools are automating labor-intensive production tasks such as CGI creation, video editing, and sound design. This transformation reduces costs, accelerates timelines, and allows teams to focus on refining creative vision.

3. **Delivering Hyper-Personalized Experiences**: By analyzing audience preferences and behavior, GenAI enables the creation of tailored content, personalized recommendations, and interactive storytelling. This fosters deeper audience engagement and builds long-term viewer loyalty.

4. **Addressing Ethical and Operational Challenges**: The integration of GenAI in entertainment requires robust frameworks to tackle ethical concerns like content authenticity, bias, and copyright infringement. Transparency, fairness, and compliance are essential to building trust and ensuring responsible AI use.

5. **Evolving Workforce and New Opportunities**: As GenAI reshapes workflows, professionals must adapt by developing hybrid skills that blend technical expertise with creative insight. New roles such as AI Content Strategist, Virtual Production Manager, and Ethical AI Consultant are emerging, redefining career paths in the industry.

The integration of GenAI is not just a technological shift but a creative evolution that demands strategic planning and ethical foresight. By embracing these tools responsibly and fostering collaboration between human talent and AI, organizations can unlock new possibilities in storytelling and audience engagement, shaping the future of entertainment and media.

CHAPTER 11: ENERGY AND UTILITIES

Introduction to GenAI in Energy and Utilities

The energy and utilities sector is the lifeblood of modern economies, providing the critical resources that power industries, homes, and infrastructure. As global energy demands rise, this sector faces increasing pressure to enhance efficiency, integrate renewable energy sources, and reduce carbon emissions. Balancing reliability, affordability, and sustainability has become a defining challenge for energy providers, utilities, and policymakers worldwide.

High-Level Explanation of GenAI's Relevance

GenAI is emerging as a transformative tool in addressing the multifaceted challenges of the energy and utilities sector. By leveraging advanced algorithms and machine learning models, GenAI provides unprecedented capabilities to analyze complex data, optimize energy distribution, and forecast demand with precision. Unlike traditional AI systems that focus primarily on automating routine tasks, GenAI introduces creativity and predictive capabilities, enabling dynamic problem-solving and innovation.

GenAI can generate detailed energy consumption forecasts by analyzing historical and real-time data, allowing utilities to anticipate demand spikes and manage resources more effectively. It supports renewable energy integration by predicting solar and wind energy output, ensuring smoother transitions to sustainable sources. GenAI enhances operational resilience through predictive maintenance, identifying potential equipment failures before they occur, thereby reducing downtime and costs. These capabilities make GenAI indispensable in modernizing the energy sector and meeting the global push for decarbonization and efficiency.

Current Challenges or Gaps That GenAI Can Help Address

Despite its critical importance, the energy and utilities sector faces significant challenges that hinder its ability to meet evolving demands. One primary issue is the unpredictability of energy supply and demand, particularly with the growing reliance on renewable sources like wind and solar, which are inherently variable. Traditional forecasting methods often fall short in providing the precision needed to balance supply with fluctuating demand. GenAI addresses this by analyzing vast datasets, identifying patterns, and generating accurate, real-time predictions.

Another pressing challenge is the inefficiency in energy distribution systems. Aging infrastructure and limited visibility into real-time grid performance lead to energy losses and increased operational costs. GenAI's ability to monitor grid conditions, detect anomalies, and recommend optimized distribution strategies significantly reduces these inefficiencies. Moreover, compliance with stringent environmental regulations and achieving net-zero goals demand advanced tools for carbon tracking and reporting—areas where GenAI excels by automating data collection and providing actionable insights.

Customer engagement remains a gap in the sector, as utilities often struggle to offer personalized energy solutions. GenAI bridges this gap by empowering providers to analyze customer data and deliver tailored recommendations for energy savings, fostering stronger consumer relationships and promoting energy-efficient behaviors.

GenAI offers transformative solutions to the energy and utilities sector's most pressing challenges, from optimizing grid performance to supporting sustainability efforts and enhancing customer engagement. These capabilities position GenAI as a cornerstone for innovation and operational excellence in the pursuit of a sustainable energy future.

Transformational Impact

GenAI is revolutionizing the energy and utilities sector by addressing long-standing inefficiencies and enabling a transition to more sustainable and adaptive operations. Its ability to process vast amounts of data in real time and generate actionable insights is transforming how energy providers manage grids, forecast demand, and integrate renewable energy sources. GenAI is reshaping energy distribution through dynamic grid optimization, which ensures a balanced flow of electricity by adjusting supply and demand in real time. This capability reduces energy losses, enhances reliability, and minimizes the risk of outages.

In renewable energy integration, GenAI provides predictive models that forecast the output of solar and wind farms with unparalleled accuracy. By anticipating fluctuations in energy production, utilities can better plan energy storage and distribution, ensuring that renewables play a more significant and stable role in meeting energy demands. GenAI also aids in predictive maintenance by identifying potential equipment failures before they occur, reducing downtime and extending the lifespan of critical infrastructure. These advancements enable energy providers to operate more efficiently, reduce costs, and support decarbonization goals.

Changes in Workflows, Decision-Making, and Team Dynamics

The integration of GenAI is transforming workflows by automating repetitive tasks and enabling faster, data-driven decision-making. Traditional processes, such as manually analyzing energy consumption trends or scheduling maintenance, are now streamlined through AI-driven tools, freeing teams to focus on strategic initiatives. Decision-making has become more proactive, as GenAI provides real-time insights and predictive analytics, enabling energy providers to anticipate and address challenges before they escalate. For example, AI-powered dashboards allow teams to visualize grid performance, detect anomalies, and implement corrective actions immediately.

Team dynamics are also shifting with the adoption of GenAI. Cross-functional collaboration is becoming the norm, as energy providers integrate AI expertise with traditional engineering and operational roles. Employees are increasingly required to upskill and adapt to AI-enhanced workflows, leading to a workforce that is more analytical and technologically adept. These changes foster a culture of innovation, where teams are empowered to leverage AI-driven insights to drive efficiency and sustainability.

The Shift in Focus or Priorities Due to GenAI Adoption

With the adoption of GenAI, the energy and utilities sector is shifting its focus from reactive problem-solving to proactive and predictive strategies. Resource allocation is now driven by data, allowing energy providers to optimize operations and reduce waste. Sustainability has emerged as a top priority, with GenAI playing a pivotal role in achieving net-zero goals by supporting renewable energy integration and carbon footprint reduction. Customer-centricity is gaining prominence, as utilities leverage AI to deliver personalized energy solutions and enhance consumer engagement.

This shift reflects a broader transformation of the sector, where technology adoption is no longer just a means to improve operational efficiency but a strategic enabler of growth, innovation, and environmental stewardship.

Top Opportunities for Meaningful Impact of GenAI on Energy and Utilities

The energy and utilities sector is undergoing a profound transformation, driven by the integration of GenAI into its core operations. GenAI's advanced analytical capabilities are enabling providers to forecast energy demand with unprecedented accuracy, optimize grid management, and seamlessly integrate renewable energy sources. By harnessing predictive maintenance and monitoring tools, companies can improve the reliability of their infrastructure while reducing operational costs and downtime. GenAI-powered consumer energy efficiency tools empower individuals to adopt more sustainable habits, fostering greater collaboration between providers and consumers. These opportunities highlight GenAI's potential to drive innovation, enhance sustainability, and ensure a more reliable and efficient energy future.

- **Predictive Energy Demand Management**: GenAI's ability to analyze historical and real-time consumption data allows energy providers to forecast demand with high accuracy. This ensures that energy resources are allocated efficiently, reducing waste and lowering operational costs. Accurate demand predictions also help stabilize energy prices, benefiting both providers and consumers.

- **Smart Grid Optimization**: By enabling dynamic grid management, GenAI ensures that supply and demand are balanced in real time, reducing the risk of outages and improving energy reliability. AI-driven optimization minimizes energy losses during distribution and enhances the overall efficiency of grid operations.

- **Renewable Energy Integration**: GenAI facilitates the seamless integration of renewable energy sources by forecasting their output and providing actionable insights for energy storage and distribution. This supports the transition to greener energy solutions while maintaining grid stability and reliability.

- **Asset Maintenance and Monitoring**: With predictive maintenance capabilities, GenAI identifies potential equipment failures before they occur, reducing downtime and repair costs. AI-driven monitoring systems extend the lifespan of critical infrastructure, improving operational resilience and reliability.

- **Consumer Energy Efficiency Tools**: GenAI enables personalized energy-saving recommendations for consumers by analyzing their usage patterns and preferences. These tools promote energy-efficient behaviors, lower utility bills, and foster stronger relationships between providers and customers.

GenAI is not just a technological upgrade but a transformative force that is redefining how the energy and utilities sector operates. By enhancing efficiency, enabling renewable integration, and fostering consumer engagement, GenAI empowers the sector to navigate the challenges of a rapidly changing energy landscape. This transformation positions energy providers as leaders in innovation, sustainability, and customer-centricity, ensuring long-term success in a competitive and environmentally conscious market.

Key Technologies and Tools

GenAI offers a suite of powerful tools and models that are revolutionizing the energy and utilities sector. Large Language Models (LLMs), such as OpenAI's GPT and Google's Bard, enable natural language processing for tasks like customer service, data reporting, and knowledge management. Generative Adversarial Networks (GANs) play a critical role in synthesizing data for energy forecasting, while reinforcement learning models optimize complex systems such as grid management and energy distribution. Platforms like Microsoft Azure AI and Google Cloud AI provide robust, scalable infrastructure for deploying AI solutions across energy operations.

Specialized tools, such as AI-driven predictive maintenance software, assist in monitoring critical infrastructure and detecting potential failures. Other platforms, like EnergyHub and UpLight, leverage AI to manage distributed energy resources, enhance grid reliability, and promote energy efficiency. Together, these technologies provide a comprehensive ecosystem for driving innovation and efficiency in energy and utilities.

Integration with Existing Technologies or Systems

Integrating GenAI with existing energy systems is essential for realizing its full potential. Energy providers rely heavily on legacy systems like Supervisory Control and Data Acquisition (SCADA) platforms and traditional grid management software. GenAI can be integrated into these systems through Application Programming Interfaces (APIs) and middleware, enabling seamless data exchange and enhanced functionality. For instance, GenAI can augment SCADA systems by providing predictive analytics that help operators identify and mitigate grid anomalies before they escalate into outages.

Cloud-based infrastructure plays a pivotal role in this integration, offering the scalability and computational power necessary for processing large datasets and running advanced AI models. Cloud platforms such as AWS and Google Cloud provide real-time data pipelines that link GenAI tools with existing technologies, ensuring continuous updates and actionable insights. Integration also extends to Internet of Things (IoT) devices, such as smart meters and sensors, which collect real-time data for GenAI models to analyze. This synergy creates a unified ecosystem where data flows freely between devices, platforms, and AI systems, enabling comprehensive energy management.

Despite its advantages, integration requires addressing challenges such as data standardization and interoperability. Energy data often originates from diverse sources with varying formats and structures, making it essential to implement data harmonization techniques. Cybersecurity is another critical consideration, as the interconnected nature of GenAI systems increases the attack surface. Organizations must adopt robust security measures, such as encryption and access controls, to protect sensitive data and maintain compliance with regulatory standards.

Technical Trends

The energy and utilities sector is embracing a wave of technological advancements that are reshaping how energy is produced, managed, and consumed. AI-driven tools are unlocking new possibilities by enabling real-time data processing, optimizing grid performance, and streamlining decision-making processes. Renewable energy forecasting models are enhancing the efficiency of solar and wind energy systems by providing accurate predictions that support storage and distribution planning. Autonomous energy systems are transforming operations by automating critical tasks, such as load balancing and fault detection, leading to improved reliability and cost savings. Innovations like AI-powered carbon tracking and edge computing for IoT-connected devices are driving sustainability efforts and enabling more responsive, localized energy management. Together, these technical trends are empowering the energy sector to meet evolving demands while advancing environmental and operational goals.

- **Real-Time Data Processing**: AI-driven tools are enabling faster decision-making by processing massive amounts of real-time data from smart grids, IoT devices, and renewable energy systems. These capabilities allow energy providers to monitor grid performance, detect issues, and implement corrective actions almost instantaneously.
- **Renewable Energy Forecasting Models**: GenAI models excel in predicting the output of renewable sources like solar and wind energy by analyzing weather patterns, historical performance, and real-time conditions. These forecasts enable utilities to optimize energy storage and distribution, ensuring grid stability and efficiency.
- **Autonomous Energy Systems**: AI-powered autonomous systems are transforming energy distribution by automating tasks such as load balancing, fault detection, and energy

rerouting. These systems enhance reliability while reducing operational costs and human error.

- **AI in Carbon Tracking**: GenAI tools are increasingly used to monitor and analyze carbon emissions across energy operations. By providing real-time insights and recommendations, these tools help organizations achieve compliance with environmental regulations and meet sustainability goals.

- **Edge Computing for Energy Devices**: The adoption of edge computing enables localized data processing in IoT-connected energy devices, reducing latency and bandwidth demands. This trend is particularly valuable for remote locations and microgrids, where real-time responsiveness is critical.

The integration of GenAI into energy and utilities is driven by cutting-edge tools, robust infrastructure, and emerging technical trends. By leveraging real-time data processing, advanced forecasting models, and autonomous systems, energy providers can optimize operations, enhance sustainability, and meet the demands of a dynamic energy landscape. These technologies not only improve efficiency but also position the sector to lead in innovation and environmental stewardship.

Challenges and Risks

The adoption of GenAI in the energy and utilities sector introduces unique ethical considerations. One pressing concern is equitable access to energy. GenAI-driven optimization algorithms may inadvertently prioritize high-revenue regions over underserved or remote areas, exacerbating energy access disparities. Ensuring fairness in energy distribution requires rigorous auditing of AI models to prevent bias and promote inclusivity.

Data privacy is another significant challenge. GenAI tools often rely on vast amounts of data from smart grids, IoT devices, and customer interactions. This raises concerns about the collection, storage, and usage of sensitive consumer information. Without robust safeguards, the risk of data breaches or misuse could undermine public trust in both AI and energy providers. Compliance with data protection regulations, such as GDPR, is essential to mitigate these risks and maintain transparency.

While GenAI offers transformative capabilities, over-dependence on AI systems can pose operational risks. Automated decision-making processes in grid management or energy distribution may fail to account for unanticipated variables, such as extreme weather events or cyberattacks. Without human oversight, these errors could escalate into widespread outages or financial losses. To prevent such scenarios, energy providers must adopt a "human-in-the-loop" approach, where critical decisions are validated by experts.

Frameworks or Guidelines to Address These Risks

Another risk lies in the potential misuse of GenAI tools. For example, AI-driven price optimization models could be exploited to disproportionately increase energy costs for specific consumer segments, leading to ethical and regulatory repercussions. Reliance on proprietary GenAI platforms may create vendor lock-in, limiting flexibility and increasing long-term costs. To mitigate these risks, organizations should diversify their technology stack and prioritize open-source solutions where feasible.

- **Data Privacy and Security Protocols**: Implement robust encryption, access controls, and real-time monitoring to protect sensitive data. Regular audits and compliance with global data protection standards ensure consumer trust and regulatory adherence.
- **Transparent AI Algorithms**: Develop AI models with explainable decision-making processes. Providing stakeholders with clear insights into how GenAI tools operate fosters accountability and builds confidence in their outcomes.
- **Bias Mitigation in Energy Distribution**: Conduct regular bias audits on AI systems to ensure equitable energy access. Integrating diverse datasets during model training reduces the risk of systemic biases.
- **Regulatory Compliance Monitoring**: Use AI tools to monitor and ensure compliance with evolving energy regulations. These tools can automate reporting and flag potential violations, reducing the administrative burden on providers.
- **Emergency Response Frameworks**: Enhance preparedness for outages or disasters by integrating AI-driven predictive analytics into emergency response systems.

These frameworks can prioritize resource allocation and minimize downtime during critical incidents.

The deployment of GenAI in energy and utilities requires a balanced approach that maximizes its potential while addressing inherent challenges and risks. By prioritizing data privacy, transparency, and ethical practices, energy providers can navigate the complexities of GenAI adoption responsibly. Establishing robust frameworks and safeguards will ensure that AI solutions not only drive innovation but also align with societal values and regulatory expectations, creating a sustainable and equitable future for the sector.

Skillset Evolution

The integration of GenAI in the energy and utilities sector is reshaping the skills required for professionals across roles. Traditional expertise in energy distribution, grid management, and operations must now be complemented by technical fluency in AI-driven tools, data analytics, and system integration. Professionals are increasingly expected to interpret AI-generated insights, make data-driven decisions, and oversee AI-enhanced workflows. This shift emphasizes the need for a hybrid skillset that combines domain knowledge with digital and analytical competencies.

Training and Upskilling Needs

To thrive in this evolving landscape, organizations must prioritize training programs that empower employees to adapt to GenAI-driven processes. Training initiatives should cover foundational AI concepts, such as machine learning and natural language processing, to demystify the technology and ensure professionals understand its applications and limitations. Practical workshops on AI tools, including energy forecasting platforms and predictive maintenance software, will equip teams to integrate these solutions into their workflows effectively.

In addition to technical skills, soft skills such as critical thinking, adaptability, and collaboration are becoming increasingly important. As GenAI automates routine tasks, professionals must focus on strategic decision-making, creative problem-solving, and cross-functional teamwork. Upskilling efforts should also emphasize ethical considerations, including data privacy and bias mitigation, to ensure responsible AI use within the energy sector.

Leadership development programs are essential to prepare executives for overseeing AI-driven transformations. Training for leaders should include strategies for fostering a culture of innovation, aligning AI initiatives with business goals, and managing change effectively. By investing in comprehensive upskilling initiatives, organizations can ensure their workforce is ready to navigate the complexities and opportunities of a GenAI-powered future.

The Potential for New Roles or Career Paths

The adoption of GenAI in energy and utilities is creating a range of specialized roles that reflect the sector's technological evolution. These roles combine traditional energy expertise with advanced AI competencies, offering exciting career opportunities. Below are five emerging roles:

- **AI Energy Strategist**: Responsible for designing and implementing AI-driven strategies to optimize energy production, distribution, and consumption. These professionals use GenAI insights to align operations with sustainability goals and market demands.
- **Sustainability Data Analyst**: Leverages AI tools to monitor and report on carbon footprints, energy efficiency, and renewable integration. This role supports regulatory compliance and helps organizations achieve their environmental targets.
- **Grid Automation Specialist**: Focuses on managing AI-enabled grid systems to enhance efficiency, reliability, and fault detection. Specialists in this role ensure seamless integration of GenAI into grid operations.
- **Renewable Energy Integration Coordinator**: Uses AI-driven forecasting models to optimize the integration of solar, wind, and other renewable energy sources into the grid. This role ensures grid stability while maximizing the contribution of sustainable resources.
- **AI Ethics and Compliance Officer for Energy**: Oversees the ethical deployment of AI tools in energy operations, ensuring transparency, fairness, and adherence to regulatory standards. This role is critical for building trust among stakeholders and fostering responsible AI practices.

The integration of GenAI in energy and utilities is driving a profound evolution in workforce skill requirements and career opportunities.

Organizations that invest in targeted training and upskilling initiatives will empower their teams to harness the full potential of AI-driven solutions. By fostering a workforce that is both technically proficient and strategically adaptable, the energy sector can navigate the challenges of a rapidly changing landscape while unlocking new opportunities for innovation, efficiency, and sustainability.

Emerging Trends

GenAI is set to play a transformative role in the energy and utilities sector, fundamentally altering how organizations produce, distribute, and consume energy. GenAI will drive the adoption of smarter energy systems, improve sustainability metrics, and create more resilient infrastructure. As the sector embraces AI-driven innovation, energy providers will transition from reactive to proactive operations, using real-time insights and predictive analytics to optimize efficiency, reliability, and customer engagement. The integration of AI into renewable energy, grid management, and consumer-facing services will position GenAI as a cornerstone of the global transition to sustainable energy solutions.

Emerging Trends and Their Potential Influence

Several key trends are emerging as GenAI continues to reshape the energy and utilities landscape:

- **Decentralized Energy Management**: GenAI is enabling the shift from centralized grids to decentralized energy systems, where local producers and consumers contribute to and draw from microgrids. AI-driven tools facilitate real-time coordination between these systems, improving energy reliability and reducing transmission losses.
- **AI-Enhanced Renewable Integration**: Advanced AI models are improving the efficiency of integrating variable renewable energy sources, such as solar and wind, into the grid. GenAI predicts output fluctuations with precision, enabling better storage and distribution planning.
- **Proactive Maintenance and Infrastructure Resilience**: GenAI's predictive maintenance capabilities are reducing downtime and repair costs by identifying potential equipment failures before they occur. This trend enhances the resilience of critical infrastructure in the face of climate-related challenges and aging systems.

- **Consumer-Centric Energy Solutions**: AI-powered platforms are transforming the consumer experience by offering personalized energy management tools, such as dynamic pricing models and tailored energy-saving recommendations. This fosters greater customer engagement and promotes sustainable consumption behaviors.
- **AI in Carbon Management**: GenAI tools are being used to monitor and reduce carbon emissions, providing actionable insights to help organizations meet regulatory requirements and align with global decarbonization goals. These tools also support transparent reporting for stakeholders and regulators.

Strategic Priorities for Organizations to Stay Competitive

To remain competitive in the rapidly evolving energy and utilities sector, organizations must align their strategies with the capabilities and opportunities presented by GenAI. Below are five strategic priorities:

- **Invest in Smart Infrastructure**: Organizations must prioritize the deployment of AI-enhanced grids, IoT-enabled sensors, and data processing systems. This infrastructure lays the foundation for real-time monitoring, dynamic load balancing, and predictive analytics.
- **Focus on Decarbonization Technologies**: Leveraging GenAI for carbon tracking, emissions reduction, and renewable energy optimization will help organizations meet environmental standards and gain a competitive edge in the sustainability-driven market.
- **Develop Consumer-Centric Energy Solutions**: Offering personalized tools and services powered by GenAI, such as energy-saving recommendations and usage forecasts, enhances customer satisfaction and builds loyalty while promoting energy efficiency.
- **Advance Energy Storage Optimization**: AI-driven models must be integrated with storage systems to maximize efficiency, reduce costs, and ensure the reliability of renewable energy sources. This is particularly critical for supporting grid stability.
- **Enhance Workforce AI Literacy**: Organizations should invest in training programs to equip employees with the skills needed to implement, manage, and leverage GenAI systems.

Rick Abbott

Building a digitally fluent workforce ensures successful adoption and innovation.

The emerging trends in GenAI are shaping the energy and utilities sector into a more adaptive, sustainable, and consumer-centric industry. By embracing AI-driven technologies and aligning strategic priorities with these advancements, organizations can navigate the challenges of a rapidly changing energy landscape. This proactive approach will enable energy providers to achieve operational excellence, foster sustainability, and maintain a competitive edge in an increasingly dynamic market.

Conclusion

GenAI is revolutionizing the energy and utilities sector, driving significant advancements in efficiency, sustainability, and innovation. By leveraging GenAI's predictive analytics, automation, and real-time data processing capabilities, organizations can address critical challenges such as renewable energy integration, grid optimization, and customer engagement. The technology empowers energy providers to transition from reactive to proactive operations, ensuring resilience and adaptability in an era of rapid change and increasing complexity.

The adoption of GenAI is not merely a technological upgrade but a strategic imperative. As the sector faces mounting pressure to achieve decarbonization goals, enhance infrastructure reliability, and deliver personalized consumer experiences, GenAI offers the tools to meet these demands effectively. However, its successful implementation requires a deliberate approach that includes robust frameworks for ethical use, workforce upskilling, and seamless integration with existing systems. Energy providers must balance technological ambition with a commitment to transparency, equity, and environmental stewardship.

Strategic thinking and adaptability are critical to realizing the full potential of GenAI in energy and utilities. Organizations must align their AI initiatives with long-term goals, fostering a culture of innovation that embraces both the opportunities and challenges of this transformative technology. By investing in smart infrastructure, empowering employees with AI literacy, and prioritizing sustainability, energy providers can position themselves as leaders in the transition to a cleaner, more efficient energy future. The path forward requires bold action, but with GenAI as a catalyst, the sector is well-equipped to navigate the complexities of the 21st-century energy landscape and deliver meaningful impact for generations to come.

Key Takeaways

1. **GenAI Drives Efficiency in Energy Management**: GenAI enhances energy distribution and consumption through predictive analytics and automation. By optimizing grid performance and demand forecasting, it reduces operational costs and improves energy reliability, creating a more efficient energy ecosystem.
2. **Facilitates Renewable Energy Growth**: GenAI enables the seamless integration of variable renewable energy sources, such as solar and wind, by forecasting output with precision and optimizing storage and distribution. This supports the global transition to sustainable energy solutions while maintaining grid stability.
3. **Strengthens Grid Resilience**: AI-powered predictive maintenance and real-time monitoring enhance the resilience of energy infrastructure. By identifying potential failures before they occur, GenAI minimizes downtime, reduces repair costs, and ensures consistent energy delivery.
4. **Empowers Consumer Energy Decisions**: GenAI-driven tools provide personalized energy-saving recommendations and usage forecasts, fostering stronger consumer engagement. These tools not only improve customer satisfaction but also promote sustainable energy consumption behaviors.
5. **Supports Sustainability Goals**: GenAI aids organizations in achieving net-zero and regulatory compliance by monitoring carbon emissions and providing actionable insights for decarbonization strategies. It positions energy providers as leaders in environmental stewardship while aligning with global sustainability initiatives.

The transformative potential of GenAI in energy and utilities is vast, but its realization requires strategic implementation and a commitment to ethical practices. Organizations must prioritize investments in smart infrastructure, workforce development, and sustainable energy solutions to stay competitive. By embracing GenAI as a strategic enabler, the sector can navigate complex challenges, drive innovation, and deliver lasting value to consumers, stakeholders, and the environment.

CHAPTER 12: GOVERNMENT AND PUBLIC SECTOR

Introduction to GenAI in Government and Public Sector

The government and public sector play a critical role in maintaining societal stability, delivering essential services, and shaping policies that impact the lives of millions. From healthcare and education to infrastructure and public safety, governments are tasked with addressing complex challenges, often under constraints of limited resources and increasing public expectations. As the backbone of civic administration, the public sector is instrumental in driving societal progress and ensuring equitable access to resources.

High-Level Explanation of GenAI's Relevance

GenAI represents a transformative leap in technology, offering unparalleled opportunities to enhance the efficiency and effectiveness of government operations. Unlike traditional AI systems that focus primarily on predictions and classifications, GenAI excels in generating novel content, automating processes, and extracting actionable insights from vast datasets. These capabilities make it uniquely suited to addressing the multifaceted needs of the public sector.

In public services, GenAI can revolutionize citizen engagement by enabling personalized communication and real-time assistance. For instance, AI-powered chatbots can provide 24/7 support, resolving queries across various departments such as tax administration, social welfare, and healthcare. GenAI can assist policymakers by analyzing extensive data to predict outcomes, identify trends, and craft evidence-based strategies. The ability of GenAI to process and synthesize information at scale enables governments to make faster, more informed decisions that directly benefit citizens.

Current Challenges or Gaps GenAI Can Address

Despite its critical role, the public sector often struggles with challenges such as inefficiencies in service delivery, resource allocation, and policy implementation. Bureaucratic bottlenecks, outdated technology, and siloed data systems frequently hinder the ability to meet public needs effectively. Citizens increasingly expect seamless, personalized interactions with government services, comparable to those offered by the private sector, but many agencies lack the tools to deliver such experiences.

GenAI offers solutions to these gaps by automating routine administrative tasks, enabling real-time data analysis, and improving interagency collaboration. For example, GenAI can help streamline service delivery by automating form processing, eligibility checks, and document verification, significantly reducing waiting times. It can also bridge the communication gap between citizens and government agencies by providing multilingual, context-aware assistance. GenAI enhances transparency and accountability through advanced analytics and reporting, ensuring that public policies are both efficient and equitable.

By addressing inefficiencies, enabling data-driven decision-making, and enhancing citizen-centric services, GenAI has the potential to transform the public sector into a more agile, transparent, and effective entity.

Transformational Impact

GenAI can fundamentally transform the way governments operate and deliver public services. By leveraging its ability to process vast datasets, generate predictive insights, and automate tasks, GenAI introduces unprecedented efficiency and effectiveness across numerous public sector functions. For instance, it can analyze historical data to predict healthcare demands, assist in urban planning with dynamic simulations, or optimize emergency response strategies during natural disasters. Governments that adopt GenAI can move beyond reactive governance to proactive, data-informed decision-making.

GenAI enhances citizen engagement through personalized interactions. AI-powered virtual assistants and chatbots provide instant responses to public inquiries, reducing waiting times and improving overall satisfaction. These systems can handle tasks such as filing taxes, applying for permits, or checking benefits eligibility, freeing up human resources for more complex cases. By streamlining these interactions, governments can deliver more responsive and citizen-centric services, strengthening trust in public institutions.

Changes in Workflows, Decision-Making, and Team Dynamics

The integration of GenAI into government operations fundamentally shifts workflows, decision-making processes, and team dynamics. Traditional workflows, often characterized by manual processing and paperwork, are replaced with automated systems that handle repetitive tasks like data entry, document verification, and form submissions. This shift allows public sector employees to focus on strategic and analytical responsibilities, leading to improved job satisfaction and productivity.

Decision-making also becomes more data-driven and efficient with GenAI. Predictive analytics enable policymakers to anticipate trends, assess potential impacts, and evaluate the success of proposed initiatives with greater precision. Team dynamics evolve as GenAI-powered tools enhance cross-departmental collaboration. For example, real-time data sharing between agencies facilitates coordinated responses to public emergencies, such as pandemics or infrastructure failures, fostering a more unified and effective approach to governance.

The Shift in Focus or Priorities Due to GenAI Adoption

With the adoption of GenAI, government priorities are shifting toward proactive governance, citizen-centric service delivery, and enhanced operational transparency. Instead of solely reacting to challenges, governments can anticipate and mitigate them through predictive analytics. Resources are allocated more efficiently, addressing pressing issues such as healthcare shortages, infrastructure maintenance, and public safety with data-backed strategies.

Citizen engagement has also become a focal point, as governments leverage GenAI to provide tailored experiences. Personalized communication, multilingual support, and real-time feedback mechanisms demonstrate a commitment to inclusivity and accessibility. Transparency is elevated through advanced reporting capabilities, enabling governments to provide stakeholders with clear, evidence-based insights into policy outcomes and resource utilization.

Top Opportunities for Meaningful Impact of GenAI

- **Intelligent Policy Design**: GenAI analyzes extensive datasets to provide policymakers with actionable insights, enabling evidence-based and inclusive policy creation. By identifying patterns and potential outcomes, AI-driven tools ensure that policies address societal needs effectively.
- **Citizen Engagement Platforms**: AI-powered platforms deliver personalized, multilingual, and real-time interactions, enhancing accessibility and satisfaction. These platforms streamline service delivery, from handling inquiries to facilitating digital applications for public services.
- **Fraud Detection and Prevention**: GenAI identifies anomalies in public sector transactions, helping detect and prevent fraudulent activities. This enhances fiscal accountability and protects taxpayer funds.
- **Infrastructure Optimization**: Predictive maintenance powered by GenAI ensures public infrastructure, such as roads, bridges, and utilities, remains functional and cost-effective. This reduces downtime and prevents costly failures.
- **Workforce Productivity**: Automating routine administrative tasks allows public sector employees to focus on strategic initiatives and complex problem-solving. This shift increases productivity and job satisfaction.

GenAI's integration into government operations and public services marks a paradigm shift in governance. It empowers agencies to operate with greater efficiency, foresight, and inclusivity, while enhancing citizen trust through improved engagement and transparency. By automating mundane tasks, delivering data-driven insights, and enabling proactive solutions, GenAI positions governments to address complex societal challenges with unprecedented agility and precision.

Key Technologies and Tools

The public sector is leveraging an array of GenAI models and platforms to enhance service delivery, optimize operations, and support data-driven policy-making. Advanced language models, such as OpenAI's GPT series, are used for creating human-like responses in citizen-facing chatbots, translating documents, and drafting reports. Vision-based AI tools, like computer vision algorithms, aid in urban planning by analyzing satellite imagery or monitoring public infrastructure for maintenance needs. Platforms such as IBM Watson, Google Cloud AI, and Microsoft Azure provide tailored AI solutions, enabling governments to deploy scalable and secure GenAI applications across diverse functions.

These tools empower governments to automate repetitive administrative tasks, analyze citizen feedback, and improve interagency collaboration. For instance, integrating predictive analytics platforms with GenAI enables public health agencies to forecast disease outbreaks and allocate resources accordingly. Custom AI applications, developed using frameworks like TensorFlow and PyTorch, allow governments to address unique challenges, from fraud detection to emergency response optimization.

Integration with Existing Technologies or Systems

Seamlessly integrating GenAI into existing government systems is essential to maximizing its impact. Government agencies often rely on legacy systems for functions like citizen records, tax processing, and resource management. GenAI can be incorporated into these systems through Application Programming Interfaces (APIs) and middleware solutions, enabling smooth communication and data sharing across platforms. For instance, integrating GenAI with ERP tools allows for real-time data analysis and better resource allocation.

The use of cloud-based platforms, such as Amazon Web Services (AWS) or Microsoft Azure, further facilitates integration by providing scalable and secure environments for GenAI applications. These platforms support hybrid and multi-cloud strategies, enabling interoperability between newer GenAI systems and older technologies. Leveraging secure data pipelines ensures that sensitive citizen information remains protected while enabling real-time insights.

Effective integration also requires robust data governance frameworks to address issues like data silos and standardization. Tools like data lakes and federated learning models enable agencies to consolidate and analyze distributed datasets without compromising privacy or compliance with regulations such as GDPR or HIPAA. By focusing on secure and interoperable integration strategies, governments can unlock the full potential of GenAI while maintaining operational continuity.

Technical Trends Influencing the Public Sector

- **Real-Time Data Analysis**: GenAI enables governments to process real-time data from various sources, such as IoT devices, public surveys, and transportation systems. This trend supports faster decision-making and more responsive service delivery.
- **AI-Enhanced Public Security**: Tools like facial recognition and predictive policing systems leverage GenAI to enhance public safety. While these technologies raise ethical concerns, they offer capabilities to preemptively address threats and streamline investigations.
- **Accessibility Innovations**: GenAI drives inclusivity by creating AI-powered tools that support differently-abled individuals. For example, voice-to-text and language translation systems ensure broader accessibility to government services.
- **Cross-Agency Collaboration**: GenAI facilitates interoperability between government agencies by automating data exchange and streamlining interagency workflows. This enhances coordination during emergencies and complex policy implementations.
- **Ethical AI Governance**: As the public sector increasingly adopts GenAI, there is a growing focus on ethical AI deployment. Transparency, accountability, and fairness are prioritized through frameworks for algorithm audits and citizen feedback mechanisms.

GenAI is revolutionizing the public sector with tools and technologies that enhance efficiency, responsiveness, and inclusivity. By integrating these technologies with existing systems and embracing emerging trends, governments can address complex challenges, streamline service delivery, and build trust with citizens. A focus on secure, interoperable, and ethical implementation will ensure that the benefits of GenAI are maximized while minimizing potential risks.

Challenges and Risks

The integration of GenAI in the public sector introduces several ethical challenges that must be addressed to ensure responsible and equitable implementation. One of the primary concerns is data privacy, as public sector organizations handle vast amounts of sensitive citizen information. Misuse or mishandling of data in GenAI systems could lead to breaches of trust or violations of regulations like GDPR or HIPAA. Ensuring that data is anonymized, securely stored, and used only for intended purposes is critical to safeguarding citizen privacy.

Another ethical challenge is bias in AI algorithms. GenAI systems learn from historical datasets, which may inadvertently reflect societal biases or systemic inequalities. For example, biased datasets could result in unfair resource allocation, discriminatory service delivery, or inequitable policy recommendations. Addressing this issue requires rigorous testing, monitoring, and recalibration of GenAI models to ensure fairness and inclusivity.

Transparency and accountability also present significant ethical hurdles. GenAI systems, often referred to as "black boxes," can produce outputs that are difficult to explain or audit. In the public sector, where decisions directly impact citizens, the inability to explain AI-driven outcomes can undermine trust and legitimacy. Establishing explainable AI (XAI) systems that provide clear justifications for their outputs is essential for maintaining transparency and accountability.

Risks of Misuse or Dependency on GenAI

The misuse or over-reliance on GenAI poses substantial risks for the public sector. A key concern is the potential for GenAI to be weaponized or exploited for unethical purposes, such as generating fabrications, manipulating public opinion, or infringing on civil liberties. Without adequate oversight, these risks could erode public trust in government institutions.

Dependency on GenAI can also create vulnerabilities, particularly if systems fail or are compromised by cyberattacks. Over-reliance on AI systems without sufficient human oversight may lead to unchecked errors, such as incorrect eligibility determinations for benefits or flawed policy recommendations. Governments must balance automation with human judgment to mitigate these risks.

The rapid adoption of GenAI may outpace regulatory frameworks, leading to gaps in compliance and governance. This could expose governments to legal liabilities, particularly if AI systems produce discriminatory or harmful outcomes. Proactively addressing these risks through robust regulatory measures is critical to ensuring the responsible deployment of GenAI.

Frameworks or Guidelines to Address These Risks

- **Citizen Data Governance**: Establish comprehensive data governance frameworks to ensure the ethical and secure use of citizen data. This includes anonymization protocols, access controls, and compliance with privacy regulations like GDPR and HIPAA.
- **Transparent AI Audits**: Implement regular audits of GenAI systems to evaluate their outputs for fairness, accuracy, and bias. Audits should involve independent oversight bodies and incorporate citizen feedback to ensure accountability.
- **Public Sector Training Programs**: Provide training for government employees on the ethical use of AI, emphasizing transparency, fairness, and data privacy. Empowering staff with knowledge fosters responsible AI implementation and usage.
- **Inclusive Policy Development**: Ensure that GenAI applications are designed and deployed with input from diverse stakeholders, including marginalized communities. This approach helps address biases and promotes equitable outcomes.
- **Independent Oversight Bodies**: Create independent regulatory bodies tasked with monitoring and governing AI deployment in the public sector. These bodies can establish guidelines, investigate misuse, and enforce compliance with ethical standards.

The adoption of GenAI in the public sector brings significant ethical and operational challenges, but these risks can be mitigated through proactive governance and robust frameworks. By prioritizing data privacy, bias mitigation, transparency, and regulatory oversight, governments can deploy GenAI responsibly, ensuring it enhances public services while safeguarding citizen rights. Balancing the potential of GenAI with ethical considerations is essential to building trust and fostering equitable outcomes.

Skillset Evolution

The introduction of GenAI in the public sector is transforming the skills required for government employees and public sector professionals. As AI tools take over repetitive tasks like data processing, form reviews, and basic citizen inquiries, the workforce must pivot toward more analytical, strategic, and oversight roles. Public sector employees need to become proficient in interpreting AI-generated insights, validating automated decisions, and leveraging AI tools for problem-solving and decision-making. This shift emphasizes skills in data literacy, critical thinking, and collaboration across traditionally siloed departments.

The adoption of GenAI demands a deeper understanding of technology, such as AI ethics, algorithmic biases, and data governance. Employees must be able to assess and address the potential risks associated with AI implementation, ensuring transparency and fairness in public services. This evolution of skillsets is not just a technological necessity but a cornerstone of maintaining public trust in AI-driven systems.

Training and Upskilling Needs

To ensure a successful transition to an AI-enabled public sector, governments must invest in comprehensive training and upskilling programs for their workforce. Foundational training should include an introduction to AI principles, its applications in the public sector, and the ethical considerations that come with it. This knowledge will demystify GenAI and foster a culture of acceptance and enthusiasm for its adoption.

More specialized training is necessary for employees directly working with GenAI systems. These programs should cover data analysis, machine learning basics, and the use of specific GenAI tools relevant to their roles. For instance, policy analysts may require training in using AI for predictive modeling and scenario planning, while frontline service employees may focus on operating AI-driven chatbots or virtual assistants.

Soft skills such as adaptability, problem-solving, and cross-disciplinary collaboration are equally important. As GenAI changes the nature of work, employees must learn to work alongside AI systems effectively, combining human judgment with AI-generated insights. Governments should provide continuous learning opportunities, leveraging online courses, workshops, and certifications to ensure that employees stay current with emerging AI trends and technologies.

Potential New Roles or Career Paths

The integration of GenAI in the public sector is creating entirely new career paths and roles. These roles blend traditional public service expertise with advanced technical skills, reflecting the evolving demands of AI-driven governance. Below are five key roles emerging in the public sector:

- **AI Policy Analyst**: Focuses on integrating AI-driven insights into public policy development. These professionals use predictive modeling and data analysis to craft evidence-based policies, ensuring that AI aligns with societal goals and ethical standards.
- **Citizen Experience Specialist**: Designs and manages AI-powered platforms to enhance citizen engagement. This role involves tailoring digital services to meet diverse needs, ensuring accessibility, inclusivity, and responsiveness in public service delivery.
- **Public Sector Data Scientist**: Analyzes vast datasets from government operations to generate actionable insights. These professionals work on optimizing resource allocation, improving program effectiveness, and addressing societal challenges using GenAI tools.
- **AI Compliance Officer**: Ensures that AI systems used in the public sector adhere to ethical guidelines, legal regulations, and transparency standards. This role is critical for maintaining public trust and preventing misuse of AI technologies.
- **GenAI Training Facilitator**: Leads workforce development programs to build AI literacy and operational expertise among public sector employees. This role supports the

cultural and technical adaptation required for successful GenAI implementation.

The adoption of GenAI is transforming the skill landscape in the public sector, requiring employees to develop both technical and strategic capabilities. By investing in targeted training programs and fostering new career paths, governments can build a workforce that is prepared to harness the full potential of GenAI. These efforts not only enhance operational efficiency but also ensure that public services remain equitable, ethical, and responsive to the needs of citizens in a rapidly evolving technological landscape.

Emerging Trends

The long-term integration of GenAI into public services and policymaking is set to revolutionize how governments interact with citizens, allocate resources, and address societal challenges. GenAI's ability to process vast datasets in real time, generate predictive insights, and personalize services will enable governments to move from reactive governance to proactive, data-driven decision-making. This transformation will not only enhance the efficiency of service delivery but also foster more inclusive and citizen-centric policies.

In policymaking, GenAI will empower governments to simulate scenarios, forecast outcomes, and assess the impact of proposed initiatives with unprecedented accuracy. This predictive capability will ensure that policies are more evidence-based, adaptive, and aligned with long-term societal goals. The use of AI-driven platforms will enable governments to engage directly with citizens, gathering real-time feedback and fostering a culture of transparency and trust.

Emerging Trends and Their Potential Influence

- **AI-Driven Urban Planning**: GenAI tools are transforming urban planning by analyzing population growth, traffic patterns, and environmental factors to create smarter cities. These insights help design sustainable infrastructure, optimize public transportation, and ensure equitable access to resources.
- **Public Health Forecasting**: GenAI is enhancing healthcare systems by predicting disease outbreaks, optimizing resource allocation, and modeling public health interventions. Governments can respond faster to emerging health crises, reducing impacts and saving lives.

- **Enhanced Civic Participation**: AI-powered platforms are enabling more direct citizen engagement through virtual town halls, digital referendums, and personalized feedback systems. This fosters a deeper connection between governments and citizens, ensuring that public voices are reflected in policy decisions.
- **Renewable Energy Optimization**: GenAI is advancing the transition to sustainable energy by analyzing weather patterns, energy demand, and infrastructure capacity. These insights enable governments to optimize renewable energy deployment and reduce reliance on fossil fuels.
- **Real-Time Crisis Response**: Governments are leveraging GenAI for dynamic crisis management, such as disaster response and recovery. AI-driven systems analyze real-time data from IoT devices, social media, and emergency reports to coordinate relief efforts and allocate resources efficiently.

Strategic Priorities for Staying Competitive in Public Sector Innovation

As GenAI continues to redefine public service delivery, governments must adopt strategic priorities to harness its full potential while addressing the unique challenges of the public sector.

- **Ethical Frameworks**: Establish robust frameworks to guide the ethical use of GenAI, emphasizing transparency, fairness, and accountability. Regular audits and citizen input ensure that AI systems serve public interests responsibly.
- **Interagency AI Collaboration**: Foster collaboration between government agencies by creating shared AI platforms and data repositories. This promotes efficiency and reduces redundancy, enabling cohesive responses to complex challenges.
- **Continuous AI Education**: Develop ongoing training programs for public sector employees to enhance their understanding and use of GenAI tools. Upskilling ensures that the workforce can adapt to evolving technologies and maximize AI's potential.
- **Citizen-Centric Design**: Prioritize accessibility and inclusivity in AI-powered services, ensuring they meet the needs of diverse populations. Multilingual support, disability-friendly interfaces, and culturally aware applications are critical for equitable service delivery.

- **AI Investment Strategies**: Allocate resources strategically to scale GenAI initiatives across public services. This includes investing in scalable infrastructure, cloud-based solutions, and partnerships with AI providers to drive innovation.

The emerging trends in GenAI highlight its transformative potential to reshape public services and policymaking. From smarter cities to personalized citizen engagement, GenAI is enabling governments to operate with greater agility, efficiency, and inclusivity. By focusing on strategic priorities such as ethical governance, interagency collaboration, and continuous learning, governments can harness these trends to create a more responsive and forward-thinking public sector. This proactive approach ensures that GenAI serves as a catalyst for societal progress in an increasingly complex and interconnected world.

Conclusion

The integration of GenAI into government operations and public services represents a paradigm shift in how governments address societal challenges, engage with citizens, and shape public policy. With its ability to process vast datasets, generate actionable insights, and automate administrative tasks, GenAI offers transformative potential to enhance efficiency, transparency, and inclusivity across the public sector. From improving citizen engagement with personalized services to enabling evidence-based policymaking, GenAI empowers governments to transition from reactive problem-solving to proactive governance.

Strategic adoption of GenAI requires a comprehensive approach that balances technological innovation with ethical and regulatory considerations. Governments must prioritize transparency, fairness, and accountability in deploying AI systems to maintain public trust and avoid unintended consequences. Investing in robust data governance frameworks, bias mitigation strategies, and workforce upskilling ensures that AI technologies are implemented responsibly and effectively.

Adaptability will be critical as governments navigate the rapidly evolving AI landscape. Emerging trends, such as AI-driven urban planning, real-time public health forecasting, and citizen engagement platforms, demonstrate the vast potential of GenAI to address pressing issues and improve the quality of public services. However, the successful integration of these technologies depends on continuous learning, collaboration across agencies, and the alignment of GenAI initiatives with long-term societal goals.

The true value of GenAI lies in its ability to empower governments to better serve their citizens. By embracing this transformative technology thoughtfully and strategically, governments can build a more agile, transparent, and inclusive public sector. As challenges continue to grow in complexity, GenAI offers a powerful tool to not only meet but exceed public expectations, paving the way for a more equitable and prosperous future.

Key Takeaways

1. **Transformative Potential of GenAI in the Public Sector**: GenAI revolutionizes public services by automating administrative tasks, enhancing citizen engagement, and enabling data-driven decision-making. Its ability to process complex datasets and deliver real-time insights empowers governments to operate more efficiently and proactively address societal challenges.
2. **Ethical Considerations and Challenges**: Deploying GenAI in the public sector requires robust ethical frameworks to ensure transparency, fairness, and accountability. Addressing issues such as data privacy, algorithmic bias, and the potential misuse of AI is critical to maintaining public trust and ensuring equitable service delivery.
3. **Skillset Evolution and Workforce Upskilling**: The integration of GenAI reshapes workforce requirements, emphasizing skills in data literacy, AI ethics, and strategic decision-making. Governments must invest in comprehensive training and development programs to equip employees with the knowledge and tools to collaborate effectively with AI systems.
4. **Emerging Trends Driving Public Sector Innovation**: Trends such as AI-driven urban planning, personalized citizen engagement, and real-time crisis response highlight the vast potential of GenAI. By leveraging these advancements, governments can create smarter cities, optimize public health systems, and enhance resource allocation.
5. **Strategic Priorities for Future Readiness**: Governments must prioritize ethical AI governance, interagency collaboration, and citizen-centric design to maximize the

impact of GenAI. Continuous investment in scalable infrastructure and workforce education will ensure the public sector remains agile and competitive in an increasingly complex global landscape.

The integration of GenAI into the public sector offers an unprecedented opportunity to improve governance and service delivery. This transformation requires thoughtful implementation, ongoing adaptation, and a commitment to ethical principles. By leveraging the capabilities of GenAI strategically, governments can address pressing societal challenges and build a more inclusive and resilient future for their citizens.

CHAPTER 13: IMPLEMENTING GENAI IN YOUR ORGANIZATION

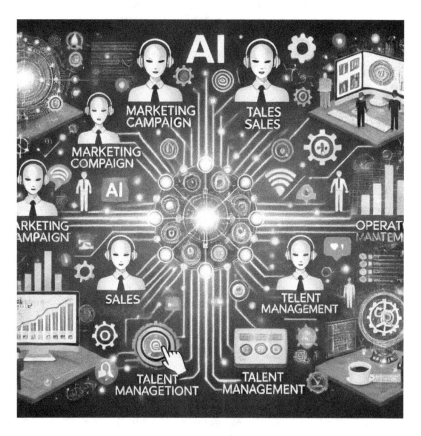

Understand Organizational Needs

Adopting GenAI is a transformative decision, but organizations must first assess their readiness to ensure a seamless integration. Assessing readiness involves understanding current capabilities, identifying gaps in infrastructure, and evaluating the organization's culture and adaptability to change. This evaluation provides a clear picture of the resources, skills, and tools required for successful implementation, reducing the risk of missteps and enabling a more strategic approach to GenAI adoption. Without such an assessment, organizations risk deploying technologies that fail to align with their operational or cultural realities, leading to underutilization or inefficiencies.

Aligning GenAI with overall business objectives and strategies is essential for maximizing its potential impact. **GenAI should not be**

viewed as a standalone technology but as a driver of strategic goals such as enhancing customer experiences, streamlining operations, or driving innovation. By embedding GenAI into the broader organizational strategy, businesses can ensure that its implementation supports key performance indicators (KPIs) and delivers measurable value. This alignment also ensures that stakeholders across the organization recognize GenAI as a tool for achieving shared goals, fostering collaboration and support for its deployment.

Integrating new technologies like GenAI into existing workflows comes with challenges that organizations must anticipate. Legacy systems may not easily accommodate the advanced capabilities of GenAI, leading to compatibility issues and additional costs for upgrades or replacements. Resistance to change from employees, particularly if they fear job displacement, can hinder adoption and limit the technology's effectiveness. Existing workflows might require significant redesign to incorporate GenAI effectively, which can disrupt operations in the short term. Addressing these challenges with clear communication, robust training programs, and phased implementation plans can ease the transition and ensure a smoother integration process.

Develop a GenAI Implementation Strategy

Creating a strategy for GenAI integration requires a structured, step-by-step approach that ensures alignment with organizational objectives and readiness. The process begins with a comprehensive needs assessment, identifying key areas where GenAI can provide value, such as automating tasks, enhancing customer experiences, or enabling data-driven decisions. This is followed by prioritizing projects based on potential ROI, feasibility, and alignment with long-term goals. Once priorities are established, organizations should outline a phased implementation plan, starting with small, manageable pilot projects to test GenAI's efficacy and refine the approach. These pilots can then inform a broader rollout strategy, scaling successful implementations across departments.

The strategy must also include resource planning, identifying necessary investments in technology, talent, and training. Risk management is another critical component, addressing concerns such as ethical considerations, data security, and compliance with regulations. Organizations should also establish feedback loops to evaluate GenAI's performance continuously and adapt the strategy as needed. By following this step-by-step approach, businesses can integrate GenAI effectively and sustainably, ensuring it delivers maximum value.

Cross-functional collaboration and leadership buy-in are essential to the success of any GenAI implementation strategy. GenAI impacts multiple business functions, requiring input from IT, legal, HR, and more to identify pain points and tailor solutions effectively. Collaborative planning ensures that GenAI solutions are aligned with the specific needs of each department while fostering a sense of shared ownership over the technology. Leadership buy-in is equally critical, as it provides the necessary authority, resources, and cultural momentum for successful adoption. Executives must champion GenAI projects, demonstrating their importance and encouraging teams to embrace the opportunities they present. Clear communication from leadership also helps alleviate concerns about disruptions or job displacement, creating a positive environment for change.

To measure the success of GenAI initiatives, organizations need a robust framework for defining measurable goals and KPIs. This framework ensures that GenAI projects are aligned with strategic priorities and deliver tangible outcomes. Below are five essential components of such a framework:

- **Strategic Alignment**: Each GenAI project should directly support the organization's overarching goals, such as improving customer retention, increasing operational efficiency, or enhancing innovation. This alignment ensures that resources are focused on initiatives that deliver strategic value.
- **Baseline Metrics**: Establishing a clear starting point for current performance is critical for evaluating the impact of GenAI. Baseline metrics provide a point of comparison to measure improvements in key areas, such as time savings or cost reductions.
- **Specific KPIs**: Define clear, actionable KPIs tailored to each project. In customer service, this might include reducing average response times or improving customer satisfaction scores by a specific percentage.
- **Regular Monitoring**: Implement a system for ongoing performance tracking, using dashboards or analytics tools to provide real-time insights into GenAI's impact. This ensures that projects stay on track and any issues are identified early.

- **Feedback and Iteration**: Continuously gather feedback from stakeholders and end-users to refine GenAI solutions. This iterative approach ensures that projects remain relevant and responsive to evolving business needs.

By incorporating these components into the implementation strategy, organizations can establish clear expectations, monitor progress effectively, and adapt to maximize the benefits of GenAI.

Build Infrastructure and Tools

Implementing GenAI successfully requires a robust technological foundation that supports seamless integration and scalability. A strong data infrastructure is at the core, enabling organizations to collect, store, and process vast amounts of high-quality data essential for training and fine-tuning GenAI models. This includes secure data storage solutions, real-time data pipelines, and advanced analytics platforms. Equally important is choosing the right GenAI platforms and models, such as pretrained models that can be fine-tuned for specific applications or custom-built solutions tailored to unique business needs. Establishing a scalable and flexible infrastructure ensures that GenAI implementations can evolve alongside the organization's growing requirements.

Organizations need to ensure that their infrastructure aligns with GenAI's computational demands. GenAI models, particularly large language models (LLMs) and advanced image generation systems, require substantial computing power. Cloud-based solutions play a critical role in meeting these demands, offering scalability, cost efficiency, and easy deployment. Whether through public, private, or hybrid cloud systems, organizations can leverage powerful computing resources without significant upfront investments, making GenAI accessible to businesses of all sizes.

Cloud computing is essential for GenAI deployment, providing the scalability needed to train and run large models. Cloud platforms such as AWS, Google Cloud, and Microsoft Azure offer specialized AI and machine learning services, enabling rapid model development and deployment. These services often include tools for managing data pipelines, automating workflows, and scaling processing power as demand fluctuates. For example, organizations can use cloud-hosted machine learning frameworks like TensorFlow and PyTorch to accelerate model development and ensure cost-effective scalability.

API integrations are another critical component, enabling GenAI systems to interact seamlessly with existing tools and workflows. APIs facilitate the integration of GenAI into CRM platforms, ERP systems, and other enterprise software, enhancing functionality and streamlining processes. Integrating GenAI into a CRM system can enable advanced predictive analytics, automated customer segmentation, and real-time sentiment analysis, enhancing the organization's ability to deliver personalized customer experiences.

Hardware considerations also play a vital role, especially for organizations that choose on-premises solutions. High-performance GPUs and TPUs are often required to process the vast amounts of data involved in training and running GenAI models. Hardware acceleration ensures that tasks such as image recognition, natural language processing, and deep learning can be performed efficiently. Edge computing can complement cloud solutions by enabling real-time GenAI applications at the network's edge, such as predictive maintenance in manufacturing or dynamic pricing in retail.

Popular GenAI Tools and Platforms

A wide range of tools and platforms are available to support organizations in their GenAI journey. Below are five popular options that businesses can leverage to enhance their capabilities:

- **OpenAI GPT Models**: These large language models are highly versatile, capable of generating human-like text, answering questions, summarizing content, and more. OpenAI's GPT models can be fine-tuned for specific use cases, such as customer service chatbots or automated content generation.
- **DALL·E**: Specializing in text-to-image generation, DALL·E allows businesses to create realistic or stylized images from textual descriptions. This tool is particularly useful in marketing, product design, and creative industries.
- **Google Cloud AI Platform**: This platform offers end-to-end tools for building, training, and deploying GenAI models. With support for TensorFlow and other frameworks, it provides robust infrastructure for organizations seeking scalable AI solutions.
- **Microsoft Azure Cognitive Services**: Azure's suite of cognitive services includes APIs for vision, speech, language, and decision-making tasks. These tools enable businesses to

incorporate advanced AI capabilities into their applications without extensive in-house expertise.

- **IBM Watson AI:** IBM Watson provides a suite of AI services for natural language understanding, predictive analytics, and machine learning. Its advanced capabilities in industries like healthcare, finance, and customer service make it a valuable tool for organizations aiming to implement GenAI effectively.

By leveraging these tools and technologies, organizations can streamline their GenAI implementations, ensuring robust functionality, integration, and scalability. This foundational infrastructure enables businesses to harness GenAI's full potential, driving innovation and efficiency across all functions.

Upskill the Workforce

The adoption of GenAI in an organization brings significant changes to the skills required for employees at all levels. Traditional roles are evolving, and professionals now need to be proficient in working alongside AI tools to enhance their productivity and decision-making. Core competencies such as data literacy, AI ethics, and prompt engineering are becoming essential. Employees must understand how to interpret GenAI outputs and use these insights to inform their actions effectively. These changes demand not only technical skills but also adaptability, critical thinking, and collaboration to harness the full potential of GenAI.

The skill shift also necessitates a focus on more strategic and creative capabilities as routine and repetitive tasks become automated. Employees in marketing may need to learn how to guide GenAI tools to create effective campaigns, while finance professionals might need to understand how AI models generate financial forecasts. Across the organization, there is an increasing demand for individuals who can bridge the gap between AI technologies and business objectives, ensuring that GenAI solutions align with organizational goals.

Training programs, workshops, and targeted upskilling initiatives are critical to address these evolving requirements. Organizations must invest in developing in-house expertise to manage and leverage GenAI effectively. This involves offering structured learning paths tailored to various roles, ensuring employees acquire the necessary knowledge and skills to collaborate with AI systems. Workshops and hands-on sessions focusing on specific tools, such as OpenAI GPT or DALL·E, can empower teams to explore real-world applications and foster confidence in using these technologies.

Organizations must ensure that training initiatives are continuous and adaptable. As GenAI tools evolve, employees need to stay updated on the latest advancements. Partnering with educational institutions, AI providers, and online learning platforms can help deliver high-quality, up-to-date training content. Initiatives like hackathons or AI-focused boot camps can further encourage employees to experiment with GenAI tools and discover innovative use cases.

To create an environment where continuous learning and AI literacy thrive, organizations must adopt a strategic approach. Below are five effective strategies:

- **Personalized Learning Paths**: Design training programs tailored to individual roles and skill levels. For example, IT teams may focus on advanced AI development, while customer service teams learn to leverage AI chatbots effectively. Personalized approaches ensure relevance and engagement.
- **AI Literacy Programs**: Implement organization-wide initiatives to educate employees on fundamental AI concepts, ethics, and applications. Providing a baseline understanding helps demystify GenAI and reduces resistance to its adoption.
- **Collaborative Learning Platforms**: Utilize internal platforms for knowledge sharing, where employees can share insights, tips, and best practices related to GenAI tools. Peer-to-peer learning fosters a culture of collaboration and accelerates collective skill-building.
- **Leadership-Led Training**: Engage leadership to champion AI adoption by participating in and supporting training initiatives. When leaders demonstrate AI proficiency and commitment, it sets a precedent for the entire organization to follow.
- **Recognition and Incentives**: Motivate employees to participate in upskilling by offering recognition and rewards for completing training programs or demonstrating AI expertise. This could include certifications, promotions, or monetary incentives, reinforcing the value of learning.

By prioritizing upskilling and fostering a culture of continuous learning, organizations can equip their workforce with the tools and knowledge needed to succeed in the age of GenAI. This not only ensures smoother adoption of new technologies but also empowers employees to unlock innovative opportunities for the organization.

Pilot and Scale GenAI Initiatives

Introducing GenAI into an organization begins with small-scale pilot projects designed to validate use cases and demonstrate tangible value. Pilots offer a controlled environment to test GenAI solutions, ensuring they address specific business needs and align with organizational goals. These projects help identify potential challenges, such as integration issues or user adoption barriers, and provide an opportunity to refine models and workflows before larger-scale deployment. Pilots allow organizations to collect critical feedback from stakeholders and end-users, building confidence and support for GenAI initiatives across the organization.

Starting with focused pilots also enables organizations to measure the impact of GenAI solutions against predefined success metrics. Whether enhancing customer experience through AI-driven chatbots or optimizing inventory management with predictive analytics, pilots offer a clear view of the potential return on investment (ROI). By demonstrating success in smaller settings, organizations can make a stronger case for scaling these initiatives, ensuring broader adoption is both strategic and well-supported.

Scaling successful pilots across the organization requires a structured approach that includes stakeholder alignment, robust change management, and a clear roadmap. First, organizations should document the results and lessons learned from pilot projects, creating detailed case studies that highlight the value GenAI delivered. This documentation serves as a persuasive tool for securing leadership buy-in and allocating resources for broader deployment. Aligning GenAI initiatives with organizational priorities ensures that scaling efforts contribute directly to achieving business objectives.

The next step involves standardizing GenAI models and processes to ensure consistency and scalability. Organizations should establish guidelines for integrating GenAI solutions into existing workflows, including data handling, compliance, and monitoring protocols. A centralized team or AI Center of Excellence (CoE) can play a critical role in maintaining quality, fostering collaboration, and supporting various business units during the scaling process. Automation tools and APIs can streamline the deployment of GenAI models across multiple departments, minimizing operational disruptions.

Continuous monitoring and iteration are essential as GenAI solutions are scaled. Organizations should track KPIs to measure the impact of GenAI across functions, adjusting based on feedback and evolving business needs. Regular training and communication with end-users ensure that employees are equipped to maximize the benefits of scaled GenAI applications. By embedding a culture of experimentation and adaptability, organizations can sustain the long-term success of GenAI initiatives.

Pilot projects provide an excellent starting point for exploring the potential of GenAI across various business functions. Below are five examples of impactful pilot initiatives:

- **Customer Support Chatbot**: Deploy an AI-driven chatbot to handle tier-1 customer inquiries. This pilot project can measure how effectively the bot reduces response times and resolves common issues while freeing up human agents for complex tasks. Success metrics include customer satisfaction scores, and the percentage of inquiries resolved without human intervention.
- **AI-Assisted Inventory Management**: Use GenAI to analyze historical sales data and predict future inventory needs. This pilot can improve stock replenishment accuracy, reduce overstock or stockouts, and optimize supply chain efficiency. Metrics such as inventory turnover and order fulfillment rates can assess its success.
- **Personalized Marketing Campaigns**: Leverage GenAI to create targeted advertising content based on customer data and preferences. This pilot focuses on enhancing engagement and conversion rates while reducing marketing spend. Success can be measured by click-through rates, sales uplift, and customer acquisition costs.
- **Employee Onboarding Assistant**: Implement a GenAI-powered virtual assistant to guide new hires through the onboarding process. This pilot aims to streamline administrative tasks, provide instant answers to common questions, and personalize training content. Metrics include onboarding completion time and new hire satisfaction scores.
- **Financial Forecasting Tool**: Test GenAI models to generate more accurate financial projections by analyzing market trends and internal data. This pilot can help finance

teams make data-driven decisions, improving budget planning and risk assessment. Key metrics include forecast accuracy and decision-making speed.

By piloting GenAI initiatives in targeted areas, organizations can identify high impact use cases, refine their approaches, and build a foundation for scaling these solutions across the enterprise.

Measure Impact and Continuous Improvement

Assessing the effectiveness and ROI of GenAI initiatives is critical for ensuring their alignment with business objectives and justifying ongoing investments. Organizations can evaluate these initiatives by measuring quantitative metrics such as cost savings, process efficiency, revenue growth, and customer satisfaction. Qualitative feedback from stakeholders, including employees and customers, provides insights into the broader impact of GenAI applications on workflows, team dynamics, and user experiences. A well-rounded assessment strategy helps organizations identify what works, refine their approaches, and scale successes.

Monitoring and iterative improvement are essential for optimizing the results of GenAI initiatives over time. As business environments and technologies evolve, GenAI solutions must be continuously fine-tuned to remain effective and relevant. Regular performance reviews, data analysis, and feedback from end-users can uncover areas for improvement, whether related to model accuracy, integration with workflows, or overall usability. By treating GenAI initiatives as dynamic systems rather than static implementations, organizations can drive sustained value and stay ahead of competitors.

Iterative improvement involves not only refining existing GenAI models but also exploring new applications and enhancements. Organizations can experiment with updated algorithms, integrate additional data sources, or expand the use of GenAI into adjacent functions. Collaboration across departments ensures that improvements are informed by diverse perspectives, fostering innovation and resilience. Maintaining flexibility and an adaptive mindset is crucial for addressing challenges and seizing new opportunities as they arise.

Regular feedback loops and adaptability to evolving technologies and market conditions are vital for long-term success. Organizations should establish structured mechanisms for gathering input from employees, customers, and other stakeholders to ensure that GenAI initiatives meet their needs and expectations. Leveraging advances in technology, such as updates in GenAI platforms or emerging tools, can further enhance performance. Organizations must remain vigilant to shifting market dynamics, such as changes in customer behavior or competitive pressures, and adjust their GenAI strategies accordingly.

To measure the success of GenAI initiatives, organizations should rely on a mix of metrics that reflect both operational performance and strategic outcomes. Below are examples of such metrics:

- **Cost Savings**: This metric tracks reductions in operational expenses due to GenAI automation or optimization. Savings might come from lower staffing needs for repetitive tasks or reduced waste in inventory management.
- **Efficiency Gains**: Efficiency is assessed by measuring improvements in processes such as response times, throughput, or task completion rates. An example is the time saved by deploying an AI-powered chatbot to handle routine customer queries.
- **Customer Satisfaction Scores (CSAT)**: CSAT measures how satisfied customers are with services powered by GenAI, such as personalized recommendations or faster support resolution. Positive trends in this metric indicate successful customer-centric applications of GenAI.
- **Revenue Growth**: This metric captures the financial impact of GenAI on increasing sales or creating new revenue streams. AI-generated targeted marketing campaigns may lead to higher conversion rates and incremental sales.
- **Model Accuracy**: For predictive or generative models, accuracy measures the degree to which GenAI delivers correct or relevant outputs. Improvements in accuracy indicate better alignment with business needs and higher value delivery.

By systematically measuring these metrics and maintaining a commitment to continuous improvement, organizations can maximize the potential of GenAI, adapt to changing circumstances, and ensure long-term success.

Key Takeaways

1. **Assess Organizational Readiness**: Understanding your organization's preparedness for GenAI adoption is the first

step. By evaluating infrastructure, skillsets, and cultural readiness, you can ensure a smoother integration of AI into existing workflows and align initiatives with overall business strategies.

2. **Develop a Clear Implementation Strategy**: A structured approach to GenAI adoption is critical for success. This includes setting measurable goals, securing leadership buy-in, and fostering cross-functional collaboration to ensure alignment across all business units.

3. **Invest in Infrastructure and Upskilling**: Building the right technological foundation and enhancing workforce capabilities are pivotal. This involves leveraging robust data platforms, integrating advanced GenAI tools, and equipping teams with the skills needed to operate and optimize these systems.

4. **Pilot, Scale, and Measure Success**: Start with small-scale pilot projects to test use cases and gain stakeholder confidence before scaling across the organization. Use metrics like cost savings, efficiency gains, and customer satisfaction to measure impact and refine initiatives.

5. **Commit to Continuous Improvement**: GenAI implementation is a dynamic process that requires regular monitoring, feedback loops, and adaptability. By iterating on models and strategies in response to evolving technologies and market conditions, organizations can sustain and amplify the value of their GenAI investments.

CHAPTER 14: FUTURE TRENDS

Introduction to Future Trends in GenAI

GenAI is advancing at an unprecedented pace, reshaping industries and redefining the capabilities of artificial intelligence. From text generation to complex multimodal models that integrate text, image, and video, GenAI is rapidly evolving, driven by breakthroughs in machine learning architectures, access to vast datasets, and the increasing power of computational resources. These innovations are enabling GenAI to achieve levels of creativity, accuracy, and adaptability that were unimaginable just a few years ago, positioning it as a cornerstone of the next technological revolution.

Understanding future trends in GenAI is crucial for organizations aiming to maintain a competitive edge. The rapid evolution of this technology introduces both opportunities and challenges that require proactive strategic planning. Businesses need to anticipate how advancements in GenAI will affect their industries, customer behaviors, and operational models. Organizations leveraging early insights into advancements like real-time adaptive AI or next-generation multimodal models can harness these tools to create differentiated offerings, streamline operations, and enhance customer experiences. Missing these trends could leave companies struggling to compete in an increasingly AI-driven market.

Strategic decision-making in the age of GenAI also requires a forward-thinking approach to integration and governance. As GenAI technologies become more sophisticated, they bring with them complexities in areas such as ethics, data security, and scalability. Organizations that understand these trends will not only be able to implement GenAI effectively but also address the broader implications of its adoption, such as workforce transformation, regulatory compliance, and customer trust. By staying ahead of future trends, businesses can ensure they are not just participants in the GenAI revolution but leaders shaping its trajectory.

Technological Advancements

The field of GenAI is being propelled forward by groundbreaking advancements in machine learning, neural networks, and quantum computing. Machine learning techniques are becoming more sophisticated, enabling AI systems to process and analyze complex datasets with increasing speed and accuracy. Neural networks, particularly deep learning architectures, are expanding in scale and complexity, driving the development of more powerful and nuanced models. At the frontier, quantum computing holds transformative potential for GenAI, offering exponential gains in computational power that could accelerate training processes and unlock capabilities currently constrained by traditional computing resources.

A significant leap in neural network design is the refinement of architectures like transformers. Models based on transformers, such as GPT-4 and GPT-5, continue to set new benchmarks in natural language understanding and generation. These architectures are becoming more efficient, allowing them to handle larger datasets and achieve greater context awareness. Innovations in sparse attention mechanisms are enabling neural networks to prioritize the most relevant data points, improving their efficiency and making them more adaptable for real-world applications.

Quantum computing, while still in its nascent stages, is already showing promise in tackling the computational bottlenecks of

GenAI. Quantum algorithms can optimize complex neural networks, reduce energy consumption, and speed up model training significantly. As quantum technologies mature, they will likely redefine the boundaries of what GenAI can achieve, opening possibilities for real-time simulations, hyper-personalized experiences, and breakthroughs in areas like drug discovery and climate modeling.

Emerging capabilities in GenAI are further broadening its scope. Multimodal models, which integrate text, images, audio, and video into a single framework, are becoming increasingly advanced. These models can process and generate content across multiple formats simultaneously, enabling seamless transitions between media types. A single multimodal AI could generate a marketing video based on a text prompt while also producing an audio voiceover and accompanying graphics. This capability has transformative potential for industries like entertainment, education, and marketing.

Real-time learning is another groundbreaking development in GenAI. Unlike traditional AI models, which require retraining to adapt to new information, real-time learning algorithms can update themselves dynamically as they process data. This allows GenAI systems to respond instantly to changes in their environment, making them invaluable for applications like autonomous vehicles, real-time translation, and adaptive customer service bots. Real-time learning significantly enhances the relevance and accuracy of GenAI outputs, ensuring that systems stay current in fast-changing scenarios.

Adaptive algorithms are also shaping the future of GenAI. These algorithms enable models to fine-tune their behavior based on user feedback and contextual cues, creating personalized and context-aware outputs. An AI writing assistant could learn an individual user's tone and style preferences over time, tailoring its suggestions to match their unique voice. This adaptability makes GenAI more user-centric, enhancing its effectiveness and adoption across diverse industries.

Core technologies like Generative Adversarial Networks (GANs) and advanced transformers are playing a pivotal role in shaping the trajectory of GenAI. GANs, which pit two neural networks against each other to improve output quality, continue to advance in their ability to generate hyper-realistic images, videos, and even synthetic data. These innovations are being used in fields ranging from creative arts to medical research, where GANs are employed to generate realistic anatomical images for training purposes.

Transformers, the backbone of many state-of-the-art GenAI models, are becoming more efficient and versatile. Innovations like sparse transformers and hybrid architectures are reducing the computational overhead of these models while enhancing their performance. These advancements enable transformers to process larger datasets and achieve greater accuracy in tasks like language translation, sentiment analysis, and predictive modeling. Together, GANs and transformers are not only pushing the boundaries of GenAI capabilities but also democratizing access to advanced AI tools by improving their scalability and efficiency.

Industry Specific Impacts

GenAI is poised to revolutionize a wide array of industries by introducing transformative capabilities that were once deemed futuristic. In **healthcare**, GenAI is enabling breakthroughs in personalized medicine and advanced diagnostics. By analyzing complex datasets, GenAI can tailor treatments to individual patients, optimize clinical trials, and enhance medical imaging. In **retail**, GenAI is reshaping customer engagement with AI-generated content, personalized shopping experiences, and inventory optimization. **Financial Services** is being transformed through enhanced fraud detection, algorithmic trading, and customer service automation. Meanwhile, **manufacturing** is benefiting from predictive maintenance and process optimization, reducing downtime and costs. The **entertainment** industry is seeing an explosion of AI-generated content, from virtual actors to immersive gaming experiences, revolutionizing creative workflows and audience engagement.

These advancements are not just reshaping industry practices but are also creating entirely new opportunities for innovation. GenAI is making it possible to integrate real-time data analysis into decision-making processes, enabling organizations to remain agile in rapidly changing environments. The shift towards automation and hyper-personalization is expected to redefine customer expectations, workforce roles, and business models across sectors. Below are specific examples that illustrate how GenAI is anticipated to drive industry-specific transformations:

- **Personalized Medicine in Healthcare**: GenAI models can analyze genetic, clinical, and lifestyle data to create highly individualized treatment plans. AI can recommend specific medications or therapies based on a patient's unique genetic profile, reducing adverse reactions and improving outcomes.

GenAI can simulate drug interactions and assist in designing tailored therapeutic solutions.

- **AI-Generated Content in Marketing**: Marketing teams can leverage GenAI to create customized advertisements, social media posts, and product descriptions. These AI-generated assets align with brand messaging while dynamically adapting to audience preferences. An AI tool could generate hundreds of ad variations tailored to different customer segments, improving engagement and conversion rates.

- **Predictive Maintenance in Manufacturing**: GenAI systems analyze sensor data and operational logs to predict equipment failures before they occur. This proactive approach reduces downtime, extends the lifespan of machinery, and saves costs. A factory could use GenAI to monitor the performance of critical equipment and schedule maintenance only when needed.

- **AI-Driven Fraud Detection in Finance**: GenAI enhances fraud detection by analyzing transaction patterns in real-time to identify anomalies and flag suspicious activities. By using advanced algorithms, GenAI can detect even subtle fraudulent behavior that traditional methods might miss, safeguarding financial institutions and their customers.

- **Immersive Experiences in Entertainment**: GenAI is enabling the creation of hyper-realistic virtual worlds and AI-generated characters for movies and video games. GenAI tools can generate lifelike animations and dialogue, reducing production timelines and costs while offering audiences unique, interactive experiences.

These examples illustrate the profound impact GenAI will have across industries. By embracing these advancements, businesses can unlock unprecedented efficiencies, deliver superior customer experiences, and drive innovation at scale.

Ethical and Regulatory Challenges

The rise of GenAI introduces profound ethical dilemmas, including the perpetuation of biases, misuse of generative content, and privacy breaches. AI bias arises when algorithms inadvertently replicate societal inequities present in their training data, leading to discriminatory outcomes. Biased hiring tools could favor certain demographics over others, undermining fairness. The misuse of generative content poses significant risks, including the creation of deepfakes and other malicious applications. These capabilities could erode trust in digital ecosystems and amplify societal harm. Privacy concerns are also heightened as GenAI requires vast amounts of data, often including sensitive personal information. Without robust safeguards, this could lead to unauthorized access or exploitation of individual data.

To address these challenges, organizations must adopt ethical frameworks that prioritize fairness, transparency, and accountability. Building AI systems with diverse and representative datasets is essential to mitigating bias. Clear guidelines for content authenticity can help combat the misuse of generative capabilities, while advanced encryption and secure data practices can safeguard privacy. Ethical considerations must be integral to every stage of GenAI development, from model training to deployment, ensuring that AI technologies benefit society without unintended harm.

As GenAI becomes more pervasive, the evolution of AI regulations is inevitable. Governments and regulatory bodies worldwide are developing frameworks to ensure the responsible use of AI. Initiatives such as the European Union's AI Act aim to classify AI systems based on risk and impose specific obligations, such as transparency and accountability, on high-risk applications. Data protection laws like the GDPR are also expanding their scope to address the unique challenges posed by GenAI. These frameworks emphasize the importance of ethical AI deployment, balancing innovation with societal welfare.

Businesses must anticipate these regulatory developments and proactively adapt their practices to remain compliant. Establishing governance structures, such as AI ethics committees, can help organizations navigate the evolving regulatory landscape. Organizations should also invest in compliance audits and impact assessments to identify and mitigate risks associated with AI deployment. Collaboration with regulators, industry groups, and civil society will be critical in shaping policies that support both innovation and accountability.

To stay ahead of compliance requirements, businesses should integrate regulatory foresight into their strategic planning. This involves monitoring emerging policies, training employees on legal and ethical standards, and implementing adaptive systems that can evolve with new mandates. Organizations should also leverage technology to streamline compliance processes, such as using AI tools for data governance and reporting. A proactive approach to compliance not only minimizes legal risks but also builds trust with stakeholders, positioning companies as responsible innovators in the AI landscape.

By addressing ethical and regulatory challenges head-on, businesses can harness the transformative potential of GenAI while mitigating risks. The interplay of ethical foresight, robust governance, and regulatory adaptability will define the success of GenAI adoption in the coming years, ensuring that this groundbreaking technology is deployed responsibly and sustainably.

The Future Workforce and GenAI

GenAI is poised to dramatically reshape the workforce by transforming existing job roles and redefining skill requirements across industries. Tasks traditionally reliant on manual effort, such as data analysis, content creation, and customer interaction, are increasingly being augmented by AI, allowing workers to focus on higher-value activities like strategy, innovation, and decision-making. This shift demands new competencies, such as proficiency in AI tools, data literacy, and a deep understanding of how to collaborate effectively with AI systems. Job descriptions will evolve to include hybrid roles where humans and AI complement each other, emphasizing creativity, critical thinking, and adaptability over routine task execution.

The democratization of AI tools will also lead to a broader adoption of GenAI across non-technical roles, requiring professionals in diverse fields to integrate AI into their workflows. Marketers will need to leverage AI for personalized campaigns, while HR specialists will employ AI to enhance talent acquisition and engagement. As automation continues to permeate industries, upskilling and reskilling initiatives will be paramount to ensure the workforce remains competitive and capable of thriving in an AI-augmented landscape.

The rise of GenAI will also drive the creation of new professions that focus on AI governance, ethical AI auditing, and GenAI model optimization. **AI governance specialists** will be responsible for establishing and maintaining policies that ensure ethical and compliant AI use within organizations. These professionals will collaborate with legal, IT, and business teams to navigate the complex regulatory environment and align AI practices with corporate values. Ethical AI auditors, on the other hand, will focus on identifying and mitigating biases, ensuring fairness, and safeguarding against unintended consequences of AI deployment. Their expertise will be crucial in building trust among stakeholders and consumers.

GenAI model optimizers will specialize in fine-tuning AI systems for specific use cases, maximizing performance, and ensuring scalability. These roles will require a combination of technical expertise in machine learning and domain-specific knowledge to tailor AI applications effectively. Roles such as **AI trainers and explainability specialists** will emerge to bridge the gap between AI systems and end-users, ensuring that AI outputs are interpretable, reliable, and aligned with business objectives. The future workforce will increasingly revolve around such specialized roles, underscoring the importance of fostering AI expertise across all levels of the organization.

Workforce adaptability and lifelong learning will be essential strategies to navigate this transformation. Organizations must create a culture of continuous learning, encouraging employees to embrace AI as a tool for professional growth rather than a threat to job security. Initiatives such as AI literacy programs, personalized learning pathways, and collaborative workshops can equip workers with the skills needed to succeed in an AI-driven environment. Businesses should also partner with educational institutions and industry groups to develop training programs that address emerging skill gaps and prepare future generations for AI-centric careers.

Empowering employees with the mindset and tools to adapt to rapid technological changes will be crucial for long-term success. Regular assessments of workforce readiness and targeted upskilling investments can help organizations stay competitive in a dynamic market. By aligning workforce development with AI strategy, companies can unlock the full potential of GenAI while fostering an agile, resilient, and future-ready workforce.

Emerging Business Models and Opportunities

GenAI is ushering in a new era of innovation, enabling businesses to explore revenue streams and opportunities that were previously unattainable. Subscription-based AI services are emerging as a major trend, offering tools for content creation, predictive analytics, and decision support through tiered pricing models. These services democratize access to powerful AI capabilities, allowing companies of all sizes to incorporate cutting-edge tools into their workflows without significant upfront investment. AI-powered marketplaces are becoming key platforms for creating and monetizing AI-driven products, such as synthetic media, dynamic advertising assets, and custom-trained models tailored to specific industries.

In addition to direct revenue streams, GenAI is driving new opportunities in operational efficiency and value chain optimization. Companies are leveraging AI-generated insights to predict consumer demand, optimize inventory, and streamline supply chain operations. These efficiencies not only reduce costs but also enable businesses to allocate resources toward innovation and strategic growth. Industries like entertainment and healthcare are seeing the rise of monetized AI applications, such as virtual assistants and AI-enhanced simulations, which deliver transformative value while creating new income sources.

GenAI is also redefining customer engagement models by enabling hyper-personalized content and predictive analytics. Businesses can now anticipate customer needs and preferences with unprecedented accuracy, offering tailored experiences that boost loyalty and retention. E-commerce platforms can dynamically adjust product recommendations, while media companies create AI-curated content that aligns with individual viewer interests. Predictive capabilities allow companies to engage customers proactively, identifying potential pain points or opportunities for interaction before they arise. This level of customization drives not only satisfaction but also higher conversion rates and long-term customer relationships.

The collaborative ecosystems emerging around GenAI are equally transformative, as partnerships and co-development initiatives blur traditional industry boundaries. Companies are forming alliances to integrate AI expertise with domain knowledge, fostering innovation across sectors. A retail brand might partner with an AI company to develop a proprietary personalization engine, while a financial institution collaborates with an AI startup to create advanced fraud detection algorithms. These ecosystems amplify the capabilities of all participants, accelerating progress and expanding the potential applications of GenAI.

Beyond industry-specific applications, GenAI partnerships are creating entirely new paradigms of collaboration. Open-source communities and shared data initiatives are driving innovation by pooling resources and expertise, enabling businesses to address complex challenges collectively. These ecosystems are not just about technology but also about shared values, such as transparency, inclusivity, and ethical AI practices. They offer a sustainable path for leveraging AI at scale while fostering trust and accountability among stakeholders.

The following are examples of business models that could emerge as GenAI continues to evolve:

1. **AI-as-a-Service (AIaaS)**: Businesses can offer AI tools, such as text generation, image synthesis, and real-time data analysis, through subscription platforms. These services allow users to access advanced AI capabilities without requiring in-house expertise or infrastructure, enabling small and medium-sized enterprises (SMEs) to compete with larger organizations.

2. **Dynamic Content Marketplaces**: Platforms that host and sell AI-generated assets, such as digital art, music, and 3D models, can provide creators with new avenues for monetization. These marketplaces offer buyers a vast array of customizable, high-quality content at a fraction of traditional production costs.

3. **Personalized Health Platforms**: Leveraging GenAI, these platforms could offer tailored healthcare solutions, such as AI-generated treatment plans, nutrition recommendations, or mental health support. By analyzing individual health data, these models enhance outcomes and patient satisfaction while opening doors to subscription-based healthcare services.

4. **Adaptive Learning Systems**: AI-powered education platforms can dynamically adjust content and teaching styles based on individual learner profiles. These systems create personalized learning experiences that improve retention and engagement, appealing to both traditional educational institutions and corporate training programs.

5. **AI-Integrated Ecosystems**: Companies can build integrated ecosystems where GenAI enhances multiple business functions simultaneously. A retail ecosystem might use AI for personalized shopping experiences, dynamic pricing strategies, and logistics optimization, driving holistic growth and operational efficiency.

The emergence of these models underscores the boundless potential of GenAI to reshape industries, create value, and drive innovation. As organizations explore these opportunities, they must remain agile and forward-thinking to stay ahead in an increasingly competitive landscape.

Strategic Recommendations for Organizations

To effectively prepare for and capitalize on the transformative trends in GenAI, organizations must adopt a forward-looking and proactive approach. This begins with building a comprehensive understanding of how emerging GenAI technologies align with their long-term business objectives. Companies should establish dedicated teams or departments focused on monitoring technological advancements, assessing their potential impacts, and identifying opportunities for implementation. **Equally important is fostering a culture of adaptability, where employees are encouraged to embrace innovation and learn new skills to stay relevant in an AI-driven workplace.**

In addition to embracing technology, organizations must also develop a robust framework for strategic experimentation and execution. Starting with small-scale pilots allows companies to validate GenAI applications, measure their impact, and fine-tune strategies before scaling. Regularly revisiting and refining these initiatives ensures that GenAI tools continue to deliver value in the face of changing market dynamics. Organizations should embed ethical and regulatory considerations into their decision-making processes, ensuring responsible and sustainable AI adoption.

Innovation-driven leadership is critical for navigating the complexities of the GenAI revolution. Leaders must cultivate an organizational mindset that prioritizes continuous learning and creative problem-solving. Agile organizational structures—characterized by cross-functional teams and decentralized decision-making—enable companies to respond swiftly to technological changes. Sustained investment in GenAI research and development is another vital factor. By allocating resources to explore cutting-edge advancements, companies can maintain a competitive edge and drive meaningful innovation in their industries.

Partnerships and collaborations will play a pivotal role in navigating the complexities of an AI-driven future. Engaging with AI research institutions, technology providers, and industry consortia allows organizations to access diverse expertise and shared resources. Collaborative ecosystems foster innovation by pooling knowledge, data, and infrastructure to solve challenges collectively. Companies can also benefit from partnerships with startups, which often bring fresh perspectives and specialized capabilities to the table. Building these alliances not only accelerates technological adoption but also enhances organizational resilience in the face of rapid change.

As organizations embark on their GenAI journey, fostering trust and transparency in partnerships is essential. Open communication and alignment of goals ensure that all stakeholders are working toward shared outcomes. Co-developing solutions with partners enables customization and scalability, allowing organizations to better address their unique challenges. By strategically leveraging collaborations, companies can navigate the GenAI landscape with confidence, unlocking new opportunities for growth and innovation.

Conclusion: Preparing for the GenAI-Powered Future

The rapid evolution of GenAI technologies is reshaping industries, creating unprecedented opportunities, and posing complex challenges. Organizations that proactively adapt to this shifting landscape will be best positioned to thrive in the GenAI-powered future. Central to this transformation is an understanding of how GenAI aligns with strategic objectives, whether by enabling hyper-personalization, enhancing decision-making, or driving operational efficiencies. As GenAI capabilities continue to expand, businesses must remain flexible and ready to integrate emerging innovations into their workflows.

One of the most significant takeaways is the importance of developing an organizational culture that embraces innovation, continuous learning, and collaboration. The integration of GenAI into various functions, from marketing and finance to operations and strategy, will require employees at all levels to be well-versed in AI tools and concepts. Preparing the workforce through targeted upskilling initiatives and fostering cross-functional collaboration will be critical to unlocking the full potential of GenAI. Organizations must adopt robust ethical frameworks to ensure that GenAI implementations are responsible, unbiased, and aligned with societal values.

Investing in partnerships, research, and infrastructure is equally vital for success in a GenAI-driven world. Companies that establish strategic alliances with technology providers, research institutions, and industry peers will gain access to cutting-edge advancements and shared expertise. Agile infrastructure and governance models will enable organizations to respond swiftly to emerging trends, while sustained investments in AI research will secure their competitive edge. By prioritizing innovation and collaboration, businesses can position themselves as leaders in their respective industries.

As the GenAI landscape evolves, vigilance and agility will be essential. Organizations must continuously monitor advancements, anticipate disruptions, and iterate on their strategies to stay ahead of the curve. Those that remain adaptable, prioritize innovation, and commit to ethical practices will not only succeed but also shape the future of their industries. By embracing the transformative power of GenAI with a proactive and strategic mindset, businesses can navigate the challenges of this new era and seize its vast opportunities.

APPENDIX A: GENAI ADOPTION MATURITY MODEL (AMM)

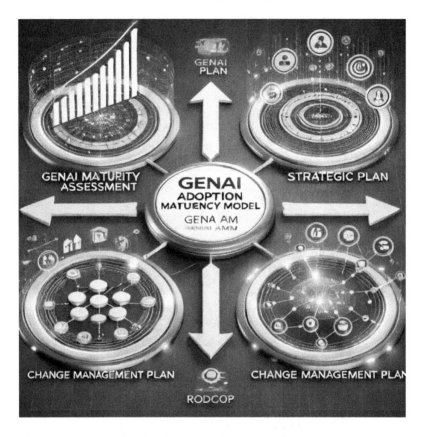

Introduction to the GenAI AMM Framework

The GenAI AMM is a structured framework designed to help organizations understand and navigate the complexities of adopting and integrating GenAI technologies. This model is a critical tool for businesses of all sizes to assess their current capabilities with GenAI, plan their adoption strategies, and optimize their use of this transformative technology.

Understanding the Framework

The GenAI AMM categorizes organizational maturity into six distinct levels, each representing a degree of integration and sophistication in the use of GenAI. These levels range from Level 0 (Incomplete) to Level 5 (Optimizing). Organizations progress through these stages as they enhance their capabilities, policies, and operational frameworks for deploying GenAI effectively. Assessment categories include:

- GenAI Model Development
- GenAI Usage
- Organizational Readiness
- Policy and Governance
- Security Architecture
- Training and Support

For each level of maturity, the model highlights associated risks and outlines key next steps to guide organizations toward higher levels of adoption and optimization.

The Six Levels of GenAI Maturity

- **Level 0 – Incomplete -** At this foundational stage, the organization lacks any deployment of GenAI. Awareness and specific policies regarding GenAI are minimal or nonexistent.
- **Level 1 – Initial -** The organization begins experimenting with isolated GenAI initiatives. Usage is sparse, and while its potential is recognized, a formalized approach or policy framework is yet to be developed.
- **Level 2 – Managed-** GenAI adoption becomes more systematic, with custom models and applications deployed on a project basis. Policies are somewhat defined but remain fragmented and incomplete.
- **Level 3 – Defined -** Organizations establish standardized processes for deploying GenAI across projects. Cross-departmental policies ensure consistency and alignment with broader business goals.
- **Level 4 - Quantitatively Managed -** GenAI usage is optimized with data-driven approaches, and performance is quantitatively measured. Policies are continuously evaluated for their effectiveness and alignment with strategic objectives.
- **Level 5 – Optimizing -** At this advanced stage, GenAI technologies are fully integrated across all business operations. The organization focuses on continuous improvement through self-optimizing models and a culture of refinement.

Rick Abbott
Importance of the GenAI AMM

A maturity model provides a structured pathway for organizations, ensuring their GenAI adoption is systematic and coordinated. This is particularly important given the complex nature of GenAI technologies, which require careful integration into existing systems and workflows.

One of the primary benefits of adopting the GenAI AMM is **improved decision-making**. By systematically evaluating their current level of maturity and identifying specific areas for improvement, organizations can make more informed decisions about where to invest in upgrades or training. This strategic approach helps maximize the potential of GenAI technologies, ensuring they are used effectively to achieve business goals.

Improved efficiency is another significant benefit of utilizing the GenAI AMM. Organizations can streamline processes and reduce wasted effort by identifying and implementing the best practices for each maturity level. At higher maturity levels, GenAI can automate routine tasks, free up resources for more complex projects, and increase the overall speed of operations. This leads to higher productivity and potentially lower operational costs.

Risk management is also greatly enhanced using the GenAI AMM. The model helps organizations anticipate risks associated with GenAI deployment, such as security vulnerabilities or compliance issues. By advancing through the maturity model, organizations can implement more sophisticated risk management strategies, ensuring they identify risks early and have robust mechanisms to mitigate them. This proactive approach to risk management is essential for maintaining trust and protecting the organization's assets.

The GenAI AMM is an invaluable tool for any organization looking to harness the power of GenAI. It guides businesses in developing a systematic approach to adoption, maximizing the technology's benefits while minimizing associated risks.

Conclusion

GenAI AMM helps businesses understand their current capabilities and provides a clear roadmap for growth and improvement. The model's structured levels—from initial awareness and ad-hoc application to fully optimized and integrated processes—allow organizations to assess their progress and realistically plan future advancements.

Organizations will benefit from assessing their position within the GenAI AMM. Identifying their current level can spotlight areas that need enhancement and help strategize the next steps toward more advanced integrations of GenAI. The benefits of advancing through the maturity model range from improved operational efficiency and decision-making capabilities to enhanced innovation, competitive edge in the market, and risk mitigation. It's crucial for businesses to adopt GenAI technologies and embed them deeply and thoughtfully within their operational and strategic frameworks.

APPENDIX B: AI PROGRAM MANAGEMENT OFFICE (PMO)

Imperative for an AI Program Management Function

Integrating AI into business operations brings with it numerous challenges. Companies often grapple with the technical complexity of AI solutions, requiring substantial investment in infrastructure and expertise. Ethical considerations also loom large, as businesses must navigate issues of bias, privacy, and accountability in AI decision-making processes. The implementation of AI necessitates effective change management to ensure smooth adoption and to minimize resistance from personnel who may fear obsolescence.

Some critical challenges with setting up an AI PMO include:

- **Resource Allocation and Planning:** Determining the ideal resources to work on AI initiatives and freeing up those resources from their day-to-day tasks.
- **Communication with Stakeholders:** Effectively communicating AI's role and potential impact to diverse stakeholder groups with different interests and perspectives.
- **Budget Management:** Ensuring AI projects stay within allocated budgets while managing rapid change in the AI technological landscape.
- **Change Management:** Leading an organization through the change that comes with implementing an AI PMO requires careful planning and execution.
- **Skill Gap:** Identifying and addressing the lack of in-house AI expertise and knowledge within the existing workforce is critical for successful implementation.
- **Cultural Resistance:** Overcoming skepticism and resistance to AI among employees who may fear job displacement or significant changes to their workflow.
- **Technical Infrastructure:** Building or upgrading the existing technical infrastructure to support AI capabilities can be a major undertaking.
- **Regulatory Compliance:** Navigating the complex legal landscape surrounding AI, including data privacy laws and ethical standards, is an ongoing challenge.
- **Integration with Existing Processes:** Integrating AI solutions into existing workflows and processes can be difficult, particularly if those processes are not designed to fully leverage AI's unique capabilities.
- **Standardization Issues:** A lack of standardization across AI tools and data formats can lead to inefficiencies and compatibility issues that complicate AI project management and deployment.

An AI PMO serves to define and oversee the objectives of AI projects, ensuring they align with the company's strategic goals and ethical guidelines. This specialized PMO works in tandem with broader IT or business PMOs (if established), acting as a bridge between AI initiatives and enterprise-wide technology strategies. Strategically, an AI PMO plays a pivotal role in aligning AI initiatives with business objectives, ensuring that AI solutions drive competitive advantage and operational excellence. Formulating an AI PMO requires strategic planning and careful consideration of the following:

- **Define Clear Goals:** Establish specific, measurable goals aligned with overall business objectives to ensure AI initiatives are purpose-driven.
- **Build a Robust AI Strategy:** Create a comprehensive AI strategy that addresses complex challenges and outlines a clear path to AI integration.
- **Develop Technical Infrastructure:** Ensure the organization has the necessary technological foundation, including data architecture and computing resources, to support the successful adoption of AI technologies.
- **Secure Leadership Buy-In:** Obtain commitment from top management to provide the necessary support and resources for the AI program.
- **Cultivate Talent and Expertise:** Invest in recruiting and training personnel with AI expertise to lead and execute an AI initiative.
- **Prioritize Ethical AI Use:** Implement guidelines and practices that ensure ethical considerations are central to AI deployment.
- **Ensure Scalability:** Build AI systems that can scale with the organization's growth and adapt to evolving AI technologies.
- **Promote Cross-Functional Collaboration:** Foster collaboration between the AI PMO and different departments to integrate AI smoothly into all areas of the organization.
- **Focus on Organizational Change Management:** Address the human element by preparing the workforce for AI adoption and managing the transition effectively.
- **Measure Impact and Performance:** Implement metrics and KPIs to track the performance and impact of AI initiatives, ensuring alignment with strategic goals.

By integrating an AI PMO into the fabric of an enterprise-wide Technology PMO, organizations can ensure that AI initiatives are not siloed but are integral to the overall technological advancement of the company.

Conclusion

The integration of AI into business processes is not a mere enhancement but a transformative force reshaping talent, technology, operations, strategy, and competitive dynamics. An AI PMO is essential in steering this transformation, ensuring that AI initiatives are in lockstep with organizational goals and values.

APPENDIX C: AI CENTER OF EXCELLENCE (COE)

Defining the AI Center of Excellence (CoE)

An AI CoE serves as the epicenter of AI initiatives within an organization. It is a centralized unit that not only fosters innovation and expertise in AI but also standardizes practices and supports the entire organization in AI adoption and integration.

The core objectives of an AI CoE include:

- **Promoting AI Literacy and Expertise:** Elevating the understanding and skills across the organization, ensuring a common language and knowledge base regarding AI technologies and methodologies.
- **Guiding AI Strategy and Implementation:** Establishing a strategic roadmap for AI deployment that aligns with the

organization's goals, and steering the execution of this strategy through best practices and proven frameworks.

- **Facilitating Collaboration:** Acting as a conduit between different departments and teams, ensuring that AI projects benefit from cross-functional expertise and insights.
- **Accelerating Innovation:** Encouraging and incubating innovative AI projects that can deliver competitive advantages and operational efficiencies.
- **Ensuring Ethical AI Use:** Developing policies and standards that promote the responsible use of AI, respecting privacy, bias mitigation, and transparency.
- **Confirming Regulatory Adherence:** Staying abreast of applicable laws and regulations and monitoring AI usage across the organization for compliance.
- **Monitoring Performance and Impact:** Tracking the effectiveness of AI projects and ensuring they deliver on intended outcomes and return on investment.

The role of an AI CoE within an organization is multifaceted. It serves as a think tank, a knowledge hub, an incubator for innovation, and a guardian of standards, regulations, and ethics in AI applications. In implementing a governance framework for AI initiatives, the AI CoE:

- **Sets Governance Standards:** Establishes clear guidelines and protocols for the development, deployment, and monitoring of AI systems.
- **Manages Risks:** Identifies potential risks associated with AI projects and develops strategies to mitigate them.
- **Ensures Compliance:** Monitors AI projects for compliance with internal policies and external regulations.
- **Evaluates AI Investments:** Oversees the evaluation process for AI-related investments and decisions based on a thorough understanding of their strategic importance and potential impact.
- **Cultivates a Responsible AI Culture:** Instills a culture of ethical AI use, ensuring that AI solutions are designed and deployed in a manner that aligns with societal norms and values.

By championing these principles, an AI CoE acts as a foundation upon which organizations can build their AI capabilities, ensuring that AI technologies are harnessed effectively and responsibly to drive transformation and create value.

Stakeholder Engagement

Stakeholder engagement is essential to ensuring the successful implementation of any CoE, particularly in the realm of AI where the impact is pervasive and significant. Engaging stakeholders is not merely about informing them of CoE activities but rather actively involving them in the decision-making process. This is key to fostering an environment of collaboration and mutual understanding.

To achieve this, the process should begin with the identification of all potential stakeholders, acknowledging their specific interests, influence, and the role they will play in the AI CoE. Following this, a detailed engagement plan should be developed, one that addresses the level of interest and influence of each stakeholder. The engagement should be multidirectional and meaningful, ensuring that stakeholders not only receive information but also provide feedback.

Meaningful engagement also means ensuring that stakeholders understand the potential benefits of the AI CoE and feel a sense of ownership over its success. This requires clear and consistent communication, transparency about project goals, and the ways in which AI CoE aligns with the organization's broader objectives. Stakeholders must be assured that their concerns and suggestions are heard and considered, which in turn, can greatly increase buy-in.

For a CoE to be successful, it is vital to calculate the financial benefits compared to the costs incurred for AI adoption. This analysis must cover both direct financial gains, such as increased revenue and cost savings, and indirect benefits, including enhanced customer satisfaction, market positioning, and long-term strategic advantages.

Key Performance Indicators (KPIs) should be established to monitor the effectiveness of the AI CoE. These metrics can include operational efficiency, error rates, customer engagement levels, and employee productivity. Assessing these KPIs pre and post-AI adoption provides quantifiable evidence of the impact on business processes. The analysis should account for the scalability of AI solutions and their ability to adapt to evolving business needs. The long-term value of AI lies in its capacity to continuously learn and improve, thereby driving ongoing process optimization and innovation.

The ROI and impact analysis must also factor in the costs of change management, staff training, and potential disruptions during the transition period. A comprehensive AI strategy includes a clear roadmap for adoption that minimizes these costs and aligns AI initiatives with business process improvement goals.

Infrastructure and Technology

For an AI CoE to function effectively, it is crucial to establish a robust infrastructure and technology framework that can support advanced analytics and AI capabilities. This framework should include:

- **Collaboration Tools:** Integrate tools that foster collaboration between AI experts, IT professionals, and business stakeholders. These tools should support the sharing of insights, model management, and the documentation of best practices and learnings.
- **AI Development Platforms:** Adopt platforms that facilitate the development, training, and deployment of AI models. These should provide support for various machine learning frameworks and libraries, as well as offer tools for version control and collaboration among data scientists.
- **Computing Power and Storage:** Leverage high-performance computing resources capable of processing large datasets and running complex AI algorithms. This may involve on-premises data centers with powerful GPU servers or more likely cloud-based solutions offering scalable compute power.
- **Data Infrastructure:** Efficient data management is the bedrock of any AI system, requiring a comprehensive set of techniques for processing, storing, and organizing data. It is critical to establish a secure, reliable, and accessible data infrastructure by implementing data warehouses or lakes that can handle structured and unstructured data, ensuring that data governance and quality are maintained.
- **Security Measures:** Apply rigorous security measures to protect AI data and models, including encryption for data at rest, rigorous access controls and authentication mechanisms, and continuous monitoring and threat detection systems to safeguard against unauthorized access and potential breaches.
- **Monitoring and Management Tools:** Utilize tools to monitor the performance of AI systems, manage machine

learning operations (MLOps), and ensure models remain accurate and fair over time

Investing in these areas will provide the AI CoE with the technological backbone required to innovate and lead AI initiatives within the organization.

Ensuring Enterprise Scalability

Scaling AI solutions across an enterprise is crucial for maintaining agility and competitiveness. To ensure scalability, the following should be taken into consideration when building the AI CoE:

- **Implement Governance Frameworks:** Develop comprehensive governance frameworks to oversee AI initiatives. This includes setting up protocols for data usage, model development, and ethical considerations, as well as ensuring compliance with relevant regulations.
- **Develop Scalable Infrastructure:** Establish a scalable infrastructure that can adapt to increasing demands without performance loss. This may include cloud computing resources and containerization technologies for easier deployment and management of AI applications.
- **MLOps Processes:** Implement robust MLOps (machine learning operations) practices to streamline model deployment, monitoring, and continuous retraining. This ensures models remain reliable and performant in production environments.
- **Standardize AI Integration:** Create and enforce standards for AI integration, which facilitate smoother onboarding of AI applications into existing systems. This ensures compatibility and reduces complexity, allowing for seamless scaling across various departments and functions.
- **Embrace Modularity:** Design AI solutions to be modular, enabling individual components to be updated or replaced without affecting the whole system. This approach aids in scaling and maintaining the AI solutions over time.
- **Address Technical Debt:** Be proactive in addressing technical debt—outdated or inefficient technology that hampers scaling efforts. Plan for gradual replacement or upgrade of legacy systems to support new AI capabilities.

- **Knowledge Sharing:** Facilitate knowledge repositories and collaboration platforms to promote the sharing of best practices and AI assets across the organization.
- **Foster a Culture of Continuous Learning:** Encourage a culture where continuous improvement and learning are valued. As AI technology evolves, so too should the organization's use of it, ensuring solutions remain effective and scalable.

By following these strategies when establishing an AI CoE, an organization can effectively scale its AI solutions, ensuring they remain robust, efficient, and aligned with business objectives.

Regulatory and Ethical Considerations

When developing and deploying AI technologies, organizations must navigate a complex landscape of regulatory requirements and ethical considerations. This includes ensuring data privacy, securing informed consent, and maintaining fairness in AI algorithms to prevent biases. Key considerations involve aligning AI practices with GDPR in Europe, CCPA in California, and other relevant data protection laws globally. Ethical AI usage also encompasses transparency in AI decision-making processes, ensuring AI systems do not perpetuate or amplify unfair biases. Organizations must establish clear guidelines and frameworks to address these issues, fostering trust and accountability in their AI applications.

Some important steps and considerations include:

- **Understand and Comply with Laws:** Familiarize with GDPR, CCPA, and other data protection regulations affecting AI.
- **Audit for Fairness and Bias:** Regularly review AI algorithms to ensure they are free from unfair biases.
- **Ensure Transparency:** Implement measures to make AI decision processes clear to users and stakeholders.
- **Establish Ethical Guidelines:** Create a set of ethical principles guiding AI development and usage.
- **Implement Governance Frameworks:** Set up structures for oversight, ethical reviews, and compliance checks.
- **Engage in Continuous Learning:** Stay updated with evolving regulations and ethical standards in AI.

- **Promote Accountability:** Develop mechanisms to address any negative impacts of AI systems responsibly.

Conclusion

Establishing an AI CoE marks a pivotal step towards harnessing the transformative power of AI within organizations. Through detailed case studies, we've seen the practical impact of AI in healthcare diagnostics and customer service, underscoring the importance of quality data, ethical considerations, and the seamless integration of AI and human expertise.

APPENDIX D: CASE STUDIES

Case Study 1: Manufacturing

<u>Taking Predictive Maintenance to the Next Level with Generative AI</u>[1]

Siemens has taken its predictive maintenance solutions to new heights with the integration of generative AI. By combining operational data with generative AI algorithms, Siemens can predict equipment failures and recommend optimal maintenance schedules before disruptions occur. These AI-driven insights help manufacturers minimize downtime, enhance productivity, and extend the lifespan of critical machinery, leading to a 20% reduction in unexpected equipment failures and improved operational efficiency.

Case Study 2: Healthcare

<u>Revolutionizing Drug Discovery with Generative AI</u>[2]

Insilico Medicine, a pioneering company in AI-driven drug discovery, uses generative AI to identify potential therapeutic compounds and design novel drugs. By analyzing massive biological datasets, Insilico's AI generates molecular structures tailored to specific disease targets, accelerating the drug discovery process. This approach reduces costs and development timelines while improving the likelihood of successful outcomes, making it a game-changer for addressing complex diseases.

---

[1] Siemens' advancements in predictive maintenance powered by generative AI are detailed (https://press.siemens.com/global/en/pressrelease/generative-artificial-intelligence-takes-siemens-predictive-maintenance-solution-next)

[2] Learn more about Insilico Medicine's AI-driven drug discovery (https://insilico.com/)

Case Study 3: Education

Duolingo Max: Revolutionizing Language Education with Generative AI[3]

Duolingo Max, the latest innovation from Duolingo, leverages generative AI to create immersive and interactive learning experiences. This advanced feature uses AI to simulate conversational practice with AI-generated characters and real-time feedback, adapting to each learner's skill level and language goals. By enabling personalized learning paths and enhancing engagement, Duolingo Max has revolutionized language acquisition, significantly improving learner outcomes and satisfaction.

Case Study 4: Finance

Optimizing Payments and Reducing Fraud with Generative AI[4]

JPMorgan Chase utilizes generative AI to revolutionize payments optimization and enhance fraud detection. By analyzing transaction data patterns, their AI systems identify anomalies indicative of fraudulent activity, enabling preemptive actions. Generative AI also streamlines payment processing, optimizing routes for efficiency and reducing costs. These advancements have not only bolstered security but also improved customer satisfaction by minimizing transaction delays and errors.

---

[3] Learn more about Duolingo Max and its use of generative AI (https://blog.duolingo.com/duolingo-max/)

[4] Explore JPMorgan Chase's AI-driven solutions in payments optimization and fraud reduction (https://www.jpmorgan.com/insights/payments/payments-optimization/ai-payments-efficiency-fraud-reduction).

Case Study 5: Retail

Revolutionizing Personal Styling with Generative AI[5]

Stitch Fix is transforming personal styling using generative AI to deliver highly personalized clothing recommendations. By analyzing customer preferences, body measurements, and style feedback, Stitch Fix's AI generates tailored outfit suggestions that align with individual tastes. This technology enables stylists to enhance their recommendations, providing a unique blend of human creativity and AI-driven precision. The result is a significant improvement in client satisfaction and increased retention rates.

Case Study 6: Marketing

Ogilvy Paris: Pioneering AI Innovation in Marketing[6]

Ogilvy Paris has launched AI Lab, a dedicated initiative to deliver cutting-edge expertise in artificial intelligence to its clients. The lab focuses on utilizing generative AI to create unique and innovative marketing campaigns. By combining AI-driven insights with creative strategies, Ogilvy Paris enables brands to craft compelling narratives, personalized content, and dynamic visuals. This approach has significantly enhanced campaign effectiveness, driving higher engagement rates and providing measurable business outcomes for clients.

---

[5] Discover how Stitch Fix is revolutionizing personal styling with generative AI (https://newsroom.stitchfix.com/blog/how-were-revolutionizing-personal-styling-with-generative-ai/).

[6] Learn more about Ogilvy Paris' AI Lab and its innovative approach to marketing (https://www.ogilvy.com/fr/ideas/ogilvy-paris-launch-ailab-dedicated-delivering-expertise-artificial-intelligence-clients).

Case Study 7: Entertainment

Revolutionizing Content Recommendation with Generative AI[7]

Netflix has developed a sophisticated machine learning platform that leverages generative AI to enhance content recommendations and streamline production workflows. The AI analyzes user interaction data to generate personalized recommendations that align with individual viewing preferences, ensuring an engaging experience for subscribers. Additionally, generative AI aids in script analysis and storyboarding, enabling creators to develop compelling narratives tailored to audience trends. These advancements have improved user retention and content development efficiency, solidifying Netflix's position as a leader in entertainment innovation.

Case Study 8: Energy and Utilities

Unleashing AI in Power Plants[8]

Siemens Energy has revolutionized the operation of power plants by incorporating generative AI into their systems. By analyzing real-time data from sensors and machinery, the AI generates predictive models that enhance energy efficiency and operational reliability. This cutting-edge technology has enabled Siemens Energy to identify potential system failures before they occur, optimize energy output, and reduce carbon emissions, contributing significantly to the transition toward cleaner energy solutions.

---

[7] Learn more about Netflix's machine learning platform and generative AI applications (https://research.netflix.com/research-area/machine-learning-platform).

[8] Learn more about Siemens Energy's use of generative AI in power plants at Unleashing AI in Power Plants. (https://www.siemens-energy.com/global/en/home/stories/unleashing-ai-in-power-plants.html)

Case Study 9: Government

Advancing Public Health Services with Generative AI[9]

The Department of Health and Human Services (HHS) in the United States has developed a comprehensive AI strategy to enhance public health initiatives. Generative AI is utilized to create predictive models that streamline healthcare operations, such as optimizing resource allocation during emergencies and generating actionable insights for policy-making. By analyzing vast datasets, the AI supports decision-making processes, reduces response times, and improves the overall efficiency of public health services, significantly benefiting communities nationwide.

Conclusion

These case studies demonstrate the transformative potential of generative AI across diverse industries, enhancing efficiency, personalization, and innovation. As organizations adopt and refine these technologies, the opportunities for meaningful impact will only expand.

---

[9] Learn more about HHS's AI strategic initiatives (https://www.healthit.gov/topic/hhs-ai-strategic-plan).

APPENDIX E: GLOBAL AI LEGISLATION

Here is a summary of AI legislation currently in place or proposed, organized by country of origin:

1. General Data Protection Regulation (GDPR) - European Union

- **Status:** In place (effective May 2018)
- **Summary:** GDPR is a comprehensive data protection regulation that governs how organizations collect, store, and process personal data of EU citizens. While not AI-specific, it significantly impacts AI systems that rely on personal data. Key requirements include obtaining explicit consent, ensuring transparency, and implementing measures to mitigate algorithmic bias and unfair automated decision-making.

2. AI Act - European Union

- **Status:** Proposed (expected adoption by 2024)
- **Summary:** The AI Act is the first legal framework specifically targeting artificial intelligence in the EU. It categorizes AI systems by risk levels (unacceptable, high, limited, and minimal) and imposes stricter regulations on high-risk systems, such as those used in critical infrastructure or healthcare. It mandates transparency, robustness, and accountability in AI deployment, with penalties for non-compliance.

3. Blueprint for an AI Bill of Rights - United States

- **Status:** Proposed (introduced in October 2022)
- **Summary:** This is a non-binding framework from the White House that outlines principles to guide AI development and use, including protection against algorithmic bias, safeguarding data privacy, and ensuring transparency in AI systems. It emphasizes equitable outcomes and individual control over AI-driven decisions.

4. Algorithmic Accountability Act - United States

- **Status:** Proposed (reintroduced in 2022)

- **Summary:** This bill would require companies to conduct impact assessments of AI systems to identify and mitigate risks related to bias, privacy, and discrimination. It aims to hold companies accountable for deploying algorithms that negatively impact individuals or perpetuate inequalities.

5. Artificial Intelligence and Data Act (AIDA) - Canada

- **Status:** Proposed (introduced in June 2022)
- **Summary:** Part of Bill C-27, AIDA seeks to establish a framework for responsible AI use in Canada. It targets high-impact AI systems, requiring companies to identify, assess, and mitigate risks, ensure transparency, and maintain accountability for AI systems that may pose significant harm to individuals or society.

6. China's AI Regulation

- **Status:** In place (as part of broader data and algorithmic regulations; effective March 2022)
- **Summary:** China's regulation on algorithmic recommendation systems, overseen by the Cyberspace Administration of China (CAC), mandates transparency in algorithmic operations and prohibits discriminatory or manipulative practices. It also requires platforms to disclose algorithmic principles and allow users to opt out of personalized recommendations.

7. Australia's AI Ethics Framework

- **Status:** Voluntary guideline (introduced in 2019)
- **Summary:** Australia's framework provides principles for the ethical development of AI, focusing on fairness, accountability, privacy, and transparency. While non-binding, it serves as a guideline for companies and policymakers as they adopt AI technologies.

8. Brazil's Artificial Intelligence Bill of Rights

- **Status:** Proposed (awaiting final approval in Congress)
- **Summary:** This legislation focuses on regulating the development and deployment of AI systems in Brazil. It aims to ensure transparency, accountability, and fairness while

preventing discriminatory practices and protecting citizens' rights in AI applications.

9. Japan's AI Strategy

- **Status:** Policy framework (launched in 2019)
- **Summary:** Japan's AI strategy emphasizes the development and deployment of AI for societal benefits, including aging population support and healthcare. While not legally binding, the framework outlines ethical guidelines and governance principles to ensure AI is used responsibly.

10. India's Draft National AI Policy

- **Status:** Proposed (under discussion since 2020)
- **Summary:** India's draft AI policy focuses on leveraging AI for socio-economic development while addressing ethical and legal concerns. It includes guidelines for ensuring transparency, fairness, and accountability in AI systems, particularly in sectors like healthcare, education, and agriculture.

This summary reflects the diverse approaches to AI legislation globally, with some countries focusing on ethical principles and voluntary guidelines, while others implement legally binding frameworks to regulate AI development and deployment.

APPENDIX F: SUGGESTED FURTHER READING

To deepen your understanding of GenAI and its transformative potential in business, the following texts and resources are recommended. These selections cover foundational concepts, practical applications, and ethical considerations to provide a well-rounded perspective on AI adoption and strategy.

Books

1. **"Superintelligence: Paths, Dangers, Strategies" by Nick Bostrom**
   An essential read on the future of AI, exploring the risks and opportunities of artificial intelligence surpassing human intelligence. The book discusses ethical implications and strategies for ensuring safe AI development.

2. **"Prediction Machines: The Simple Economics of Artificial Intelligence" by Ajay Agrawal, Joshua Gans, and Avi Goldfarb**
   This book demystifies AI by presenting it as a predictive tool. It examines how businesses can leverage AI for decision-making and operational improvements.

3. **"AI Superpowers: China, Silicon Valley, and the New World Order" by Kai-Fu Lee**
   This book offers insights into the global AI race, with a focus on how China and the U.S. are competing to dominate the AI landscape.

4. **"The Master Algorithm: How the Quest for the Ultimate Learning Machine Will Remake Our World" by Pedro Domingos**
   A deep dive into the algorithms that power AI systems and their transformative effects on various industries.

5. **"Human + Machine: Reimagining Work in the Age of AI" by Paul R. Daugherty and H. James Wilson**
   This book explores how humans and AI can work together to achieve superior outcomes, highlighting the need for collaboration between humans and machines.

Articles and White Papers

1. **"The State of AI 2024" by Nathan Benaich and Ian Hogarth**

This annual report provides an overview of the latest AI advancements, industry trends, and investment landscapes.
2. **"Artificial Intelligence and Life in 2030" by the Stanford University One Hundred Year Study on AI**
A comprehensive exploration of the long-term societal impacts of AI, with a focus on ethical and regulatory challenges.
3. **"AI for the Real World" by Harvard Business Review**
This article provides practical advice on implementing AI technologies effectively within organizations.
4. **"Generative AI in the Enterprise" by McKinsey & Company**
A detailed analysis of how businesses are adopting GenAI to drive innovation and efficiency.

Websites and Online Platforms

1. **FuturePoint Digital**
Links to blog posts and white papers covering AI from a theoretical to the practical.
https://futurepointdigital.com/
2. **OpenAI Blog**
The blog covers advancements in generative models like GPT, research updates, and practical applications of AI technology.
https://openai.com/blog
3. **Google AI Research**
A hub for AI research papers, tools, and tutorials from Google.
https://ai.google/research
4. **Hugging Face Hub**
A resource for exploring pre-trained AI models and APIs for natural language processing and other tasks.
https://huggingface.co
5. **AI Ethics Lab**
Dedicated to promoting ethical AI development and deployment, offering frameworks and tools for responsible AI use.
https://aiethicslab.com

Podcasts

1. **"AI Alignment Podcast" by the Future of Life Institute**
   This podcast explores AI alignment, safety, and ethics, featuring interviews with leading researchers and policymakers.
2. **"The AI Alignment Podcast" by Rob Wiblin**
   A discussion on how AI impacts society and the economy, with expert guests from academia and industry.
3. **"Exponential View" by Azeem Azhar**
   Focused on the intersection of technology, society, and the economy, with episodes on AI trends and implications.

These resources offer valuable insights for readers interested in exploring the nuances of AI and its applications in business and beyond.

APPENDIX G: GLOSSARY OF TERMS

This glossary provides definitions for key terms and concepts discussed throughout the book, offering clarity and ensuring a deeper understanding of the material.

AI and Decision-Making: The application of AI to improve human decision-making through predictive analytics, risk assessment, and scenario modeling.

AI Ethics: Principles ensuring fairness, transparency, and accountability in the design and use of AI systems.

AI Governance: Frameworks and policies overseeing the ethical and effective deployment of AI technologies in organizations.

AI-Augmented Leadership: Leadership enhanced by AI tools for improved strategic thinking, decision-making, and communication.

Algorithm: A set of rules or steps designed to solve problems or perform tasks; foundational to AI systems.

Artificial General Intelligence (AGI): A theoretical AI capable of performing any intellectual task a human can, with reasoning, learning, and adaptability.

Artificial Intelligence (AI): Technology enabling machines to perform tasks requiring human intelligence, such as reasoning, learning, and language processing.

Artificial Narrow Intelligence (ANI): AI designed to excel in specific tasks without broader contextual understanding.

Artificial Super Intelligence (ASI): A hypothetical stage where AI surpasses human intelligence in all areas.

Autonomous Systems: Systems that perform tasks or make decisions independently using AI algorithms.

Bias in AI: Systematic errors caused by skewed training data, flawed algorithms, or human biases, leading to inaccurate or unfair outcomes.

Big Data: Large datasets analyzed to uncover patterns and insights, forming the foundation for many AI applications.

Bounded Rationality: A decision-making concept suggesting choices are limited by cognitive constraints, time, and available information.

Cognitive Bias: Patterns of deviation from rational judgment caused by heuristics or mental shortcuts.

Cognitive Computing: A subset of AI mimicking human thought processes to solve complex problems, especially in decision support.

Consensus Building: A collaborative decision-making approach to find mutually acceptable solutions in complex or conflict-laden situations.

Creative Thinking: The ability to generate innovative ideas, often enhanced by AI's pattern recognition and ideation tools.

Critical Thinking: Systematic evaluation of information to make reasoned decisions, supported by AI's analytical capabilities.

Cultural Intelligence (CQ): The ability to work effectively across diverse cultural contexts, respecting norms and values.

Deep Learning: A machine learning subset utilizing neural networks with multiple layers to process vast data for tasks like image recognition.

Digital Transformation: Integrating digital technologies to fundamentally change organizational operations and value delivery.

Distributed Leadership: A leadership style where multiple individuals share decision-making responsibilities for greater adaptability.

Emotional Intelligence (EI): Understanding and managing emotions in oneself and others; a critical skill for leadership in AI-driven contexts.

Explainable AI (XAI): AI systems providing understandable explanations for their decisions, fostering trust and accountability.

Generative AI (GenAI): AI systems that create new content such as text, images, and music, using patterns from existing data.

Generative Adversarial Networks (GANs): A type of GenAI where two neural networks compete to create realistic outputs, such as images.

Human-Centered AI: AI designed to prioritize human needs and ethical alignment with societal values.

Human-Machine Collaboration: Partnerships between humans and AI systems, leveraging the strengths of both to improve outcomes.

Incremental Model: A decision-making method involving small, manageable steps rather than comprehensive overhauls.

Knowledge Management: The systematic process of capturing, sharing, and applying organizational knowledge, often supported by AI.

Leadership: The process of guiding individuals or groups toward achieving shared goals through vision and strategy.

Learning Organization: Organizations fostering continuous learning at all levels to adapt and evolve, supported by AI tools.

Machine Learning (ML): AI enabling machines to learn from data and improve their performance without explicit programming.

Neural Networks: Models inspired by the human brain, enabling machines to recognize patterns and make predictions.

Organizational Agility: The ability to adapt quickly to changes in the environment, facilitated by AI-driven tools.

Predictive Analytics: Statistical and AI-driven methods for forecasting future events based on historical data.

Reskilling: Training employees in new skills to adapt to changing roles and technologies, essential in AI-driven workplaces.

Scenario Analysis: A strategic method using alternative futures to prepare for challenges, enhanced by AI's predictive capabilities.

Sentiment Analysis: AI-powered interpretation of the emotional tone in text, widely used in customer feedback analysis.

Situational Leadership: A flexible leadership style adapting to team readiness and situational demands.

Strategic Planning: Defining an organization's direction and allocating resources to achieve long-term goals.

SWOT Analysis: Evaluating Strengths, Weaknesses, Opportunities, and Threats to inform strategic decisions.

Systems Thinking: Viewing organizations as interconnected systems, focusing on relationships between components.

Transformational Leadership: Leadership inspiring individuals to exceed expectations by fostering trust and creating a compelling vision.

Trust in AI: Confidence in AI systems' reliability, ethics, and transparency.

Vision Statement: A declaration of an organization's aspirations, guiding strategic planning and decision-making.

VUCA (Volatile, Uncertain, Complex, Ambiguous): Describes challenging environments requiring adaptive leadership and innovative thinking.

Workforce Augmentation: Using AI tools to enhance human productivity and creativity in the workplace.

ABOUT THE AUTHOR

Rick Abbott is a seasoned Senior Technology Strategist, Transformation Leader, and author with a distinguished career spanning over 30 years. He brings deep expertise across industries including Telecommunications, Financial Services, Public Sector, Healthcare, and Automotive. With a notable background in "Big 4" consulting, Rick has held leadership roles such as Associate Partner at Deloitte Consulting and Lead Technologist at Accenture. His professional focus encompasses IT Strategy, Business Transformation, Artificial Intelligence, and Multi-National IT Portfolio Optimization, making him a trusted voice in navigating the complexities of emerging technologies.

Rick holds a BS in Computer Science from Purdue University and has completed advanced certification in Artificial Intelligence and Business Strategy at MIT. As a forward-thinking leader, he has spearheaded business transformation strategy initiatives, application modernization efforts, and large strategic sourcing efforts. His commitment to education and innovation is reflected in his work establishing business Centers of Excellence and advising on strategic sourcing and technology enablement. Rick's AI-focused publications aim to demystify the technology and its applications, emphasizing ethical considerations and the human-centered approach necessary for AI to serve society responsibly.

In addition to his contributions to the field of technology, Rick is an advocate for holistic health and wellness. His passion for optimizing human performance extends into his writing, where he explores the science of nutrition, exercise, and mental resilience. A Jiu Jitsu Blue Belt, avid bowhunter, and experienced scuba and free diver, Rick embodies the balance of physical endurance, mental discipline, and a deep connection to nature. His commitment to healthy living informs his health and wellness books, designed to provide readers with actionable insights for improving their quality of life.

As the author of a growing series of books on Artificial Intelligence and health, Rick is dedicated to empowering readers to understand complex topics and make informed decisions for personal and professional growth. Whether exploring AI's transformative potential or uncovering the keys to long-term health, Rick's work is grounded in a passion for knowledge and a mission to share it widely.

Rick can be reached at Rick.Abbott@futurepointdigital.com or rick@360degreeview.com.